Tertiary education language learning: a collection of research

Edited by Salomi Papadima-Sophocleous,
Elis Kakoulli Constantinou,
and Christina Nicole Giannikas

Published by Research-publishing.net, a not-for-profit association
Contact: info@research-publishing.net

© 2021 by Editors (collective work)
© 2021 by Authors (individual work)

Tertiary education language learning: a collection of research
Edited by Salomi Papadima-Sophocleous, Elis Kakoulli Constantinou, and Christina Nicole Giannikas

Publication date: 2021/05/03

Rights: the whole volume is published under the Attribution-NonCommercial-NoDerivatives International (CC BY-NC-ND) licence; **individual articles may have a different licence**. Under the CC BY-NC-ND licence, the volume is freely available online (https://doi.org/10.14705/rpnet.2021.51.9782490057894) for anybody to read, download, copy, and redistribute provided that the author(s), editorial team, and publisher are properly cited. Commercial use and derivative works are, however, not permitted.

Disclaimer: Research-publishing.net does not take any responsibility for the content of the pages written by the authors of this book. The authors have recognised that the work described was not published before, or that it was not under consideration for publication elsewhere. While the information in this book is believed to be true and accurate on the date of its going to press, neither the editorial team nor the publisher can accept any legal responsibility for any errors or omissions. The publisher makes no warranty, expressed or implied, with respect to the material contained herein. While Research-publishing.net is committed to publishing works of integrity, the words are the authors' alone.

Trademark notice: product or corporate names may be trademarks or registered trademarks, and are used only for identification and explanation without intent to infringe.

Copyrighted material: every effort has been made by the editorial team to trace copyright holders and to obtain their permission for the use of copyrighted material in this book. In the event of errors or omissions, please notify the publisher of any corrections that will need to be incorporated in future editions of this book.

Typeset by Research-publishing.net
Cover layout by © 2021 Raphaël Savina (raphael@savina.net)

Reference on back cover:
Meyer, H. J. (1997). Language centres and the international dimension of university life. In D. Little & B. Voss (Eds), *Language centres: planning for the new millennium* (pp. 3-12). CercleS.

ISBN13: 978-2-490057-89-4 (Ebook, PDF, colour)
ISBN13: 978-2-490057-90-0 (Ebook, EPUB, colour)
ISBN13: 978-2-490057-88-7 (Paperback - Print on demand, black and white)
Print on demand technology is a high-quality, innovative and ecological printing method; with which the book is never 'out of stock' or 'out of print'.

British Library Cataloguing-in-Publication Data.
A cataloguing record for this book is available from the British Library.

Legal deposit, France: Bibliothèque Nationale de France - Dépôt légal: mai 2021.

Table of contents

v   Notes on contributors

x   Foreword
Philip Hubbard

1   Introduction
Salomi Papadima-Sophocleous, Elis Kakoulli Constantinou, and Christina Nicole Giannikas

7   The potential of the CEFR for languages descriptors for mediation in an ESP CALL-based context
Maria Korai and Salomi Papadima-Sophocleous

29   Multimodal texts in support of linguistic and critical thinking development in English for specific purposes
Stavroulla Hadjiconstantinou

47   Students' attitudes towards digital artefact creation through collaborative writing: the case of a Spanish for specific purposes class
María Victoria Soulé

65   The integration of assistive technologies in the SEN EAP classroom: raising awareness
Theodora Charalambous, Salomi Papadima-Sophocleous, and Christina Nicole Giannikas

89   Professional development in English for specific purposes: designing the curriculum of an online ESP teacher education course
Elis Kakoulli Constantinou and Salomi Papadima-Sophocleous

111   Technological mediation in a global competence virtual exchange project: a critical digital literacies perspective
Anna Nicolaou

133   The integration of embodied learning in a language learning classroom: conclusions from a qualitative analysis
Panagiotis Kosmas

Table of contents

151 The pragmatic functions and the interpretations of the particle 'taha' (τάχα) in classroom discourse in the Cypriot-Greek dialect: the emergence of a new function
Fotini Efthimiou

167 Author index

Notes on contributors

Editors

Salomi Papadima-Sophocleous (BA, GradCertEd, DipEd, MEd, MLit, PostGradDipCALL, and Dprof in applied linguistics – Online English Testing) is Director of the Cyprus University of Technology Language Centre, and Coordinator of the MA in Computer Assisted Language Learning (CALL). Her research revolves around teaching ESP, Greek, French, CALL, curriculum development and evaluation, language assessment, teacher education, and intercultural education.

Elis Kakoulli Constantinou holds a PhD in the area of ESP teacher education. She is an English language instructor at the Cyprus University of Technology Language Centre and a teacher trainer at the Cyprus Pedagogical Institute of the Cyprus Ministry of Education, Culture, Sport, and Youth. Her research revolves around ESP, ESP teacher education, curriculum development, language teaching methodology, and technology-enhanced language learning.

Christina Nicole Giannikas holds a PhD in the field of applied linguistics. She is an education and research consultant, she works in Higher Education where she lectures courses in Applied Linguistics and is an experienced and certified teacher trainer. She specializes in early language learning, age-appropriate digital pedagogies, digital literacies, assessment, and teacher education.

Invited author

Philip Hubbard is Senior Lecturer Emeritus in the Stanford University Language Center. Working in the field of computer assisted language learning (CALL) since the early 1980's, he has published in the areas of CALL theory, research, methodology, evaluation, teacher education, learner training, and listening. He is Associate Editor of the journals *Computer Assisted Language Learning* and *Language Learning & Technology*.

Notes on contributors

Authors

Theodora Charalambous (BA in English language and literature, MA in computer assisted language learning) is an ESL teacher in a private institute in Limassol. Her research revolves around teaching English to children and to students with learning difficulties with the use of technology. As an MA in CALL student at the Cyprus University of Technology, she has conducted research with her supervisors, Dr Salomi Papadima-Sophocleous and Dr Christina Giannikas. This research is presented in this volume.

Fotini Efthimiou has been working at the Cyprus University of Technology Language Centre as a Greek language special scientist since 2010. She holds a BA in Greek philology and a MA in the sciences of language and communication in the new economic environment. She is a PhD candidate at the Department of Education of the University of Cyprus.

Christina Nicole Giannikas, see Editors' list.

Stavroulla Hadjiconstantinou is an English language instructor at Cyprus University of Technology since 2009. She completed her Bachelor's and Master's degree in applied linguistics at Essex University, and expects to complete her PhD at Lancaster University, UK, this year. Her research interests include curriculum and material design and development, and pedagogical applications of critical thinking in education, multimodality, and digital media literacy.

Elis Kakoulli Constantinou, see Editors' list.

Maria Korai has a BA in political science, a BA in English language and literature, and an MA in computer assisted language learning. She is an English instructor. As an MA in CALL student at the Cyprus University of Technology, she has conducted research with her supervisor Dr Salomi Papadima-Sophocleous. Part of this research is presented in this volume.

Notes on contributors

Panagiotis Kosmas holds a PhD in educational technology from the Cyprus Interaction Lab of the Cyprus University of Technology, an MEd in pedagogical sciences (Università Degli Studi Roma III), an MA in new technologies in learning, and a BA in classical studies (National University of Athens – Greece). He has several years of experience in higher education and, in his PhD, has investigated the implementation of embodied learning via technology in real educational settings. He has been working as a Greek language instructor at the CUT Language Centre for a number of years.

Anna Nicolaou is an English language instructor at the Language Centre of the Cyprus University of Technology. She holds a PhD from Trinity College Dublin focusing on global competence learning through virtual exchange. Her research interests include intercultural education, virtual exchange, global competence, multilingualism, and computer assisted language learning.

Salomi Papadima-Sophocleous, see Editors' list.

María Victoria Soulé is a researcher and Spanish language instructor at Cyprus University of Technology, Cyprus. Her research interests include second language acquisition, multilingualism, study abroad, and CALL. In the last years she has been participating as a researcher in EU funded research projects: DC4LT, DE-TEL, HERO, VALIANT, and COST actions SAREP and LITHME.

Reviewers

David Barr is Head of School of Education at Ulster University, where the headquarters of EUROCALL is based. He has extensive experience in CALL publishing, serving as Associate Editor of ReCALL and the International Journal of Computer Assisted Language Learning, and is a member of the WorldCALL steering committee.

John Gillespie, Professor of French Language and Literature (Emeritus) at Ulster University, a founder member of EUROCALL, has been Treasurer of the

Notes on contributors

Association at its Coleraine HQ since 2010. He has published on CALL history and strategy, motivation in CALL, multimedia and computer-based learning environments, on language policy, evaluative concepts in translation, and extensively on the interaction of literature, philosophy, theology, and religion in 20th century (French) culture.

Dimitra Karoulla-Vrikki is Associate Professor of Linguistics (sociolinguistics/applied linguistics) at European University Cyprus. Her research focuses on Greek and English in Cyprus with an emphasis on government interpretation, language policy aimed at the law courts, civil service and education, parents' attitudes to the teaching of English to young learners, and the linguistic landscape revealed by public and commercial signs.

Elisavet Kiourti holds an MA in Computational Linguistics and a PhD on Videogames and Digital Technologies. She has conducted research in various programs (e.g. iLearnGreek, BLENDIN, InGame, PALM, Comixx, and Prison Literacy). She is the co-organizer of Global Game Jam Cyprus and Cyprus Ambassador in Women in Games. She has written books and published in international journals. Her research interests include technology-enhanced learning environments, metagaming, language and identity, cognition in gaming, and social well-being.

Elena Kkese's research interests include L2 difficulties emphasising on phonology, spelling, and writing (Cyprus University of Technology, Department of Rehabilitation, TheraLab). She is the author of Identifying Plosives in L2 English: the case of L1 Cypriot Greek speakers, and L2 Writing Assessment: The Neglected Skill of Spelling, and has published numerous journal articles and book chapters on the areas of L2 phonology, spelling, and writing.

Fernando Loizides is Senior Lecturer (Assistant Professor) in computer science and informatics and Deputy Director of the data science academy at Cardiff University, UK. He has applied research and development experience in user experience, accessibility, data science, and emerging technologies, working with both SMEs as well as large companies such as Google and Microsoft.

Notes on contributors

Georgios Neokleous is Associate Professor of English in the Department of Teacher Education at the Norwegian University of Science and Technology (NTNU). His research focuses on multilingualism, the use of the mother tongue in EAL classrooms, translanguaging, and literacy. He works with pre- and in-service EFL teachers and supervises at BA, MA, and PhD levels.

Susanna Nocchi lectures in Italian and digital technologies for language learning. Her research interests lie in CALL, particularly in the study of 3D immersive technology-mediated learning environments. Her research has also focused on the development of digital literacies for FL learning and on the affordances of audio-visual translation for FL learning.

Liana Sakelliou studied English at the University of Athens, Edinburgh, Essex, and the Pennsylvania State University. She is Professor in English and creative writing at the National and Kapodistrian University of Athens. Her 18 books with poems, scholarly articles, essays, and translations have been widely published in Greece, France, and the USA. Her poems have appeared in several international anthologies, as well as in many American journals and magazines.

Simone Torsani is Lecturer in second language acquisition and language teaching at the University of Genoa. Among his areas of interest: technology-enhanced language learning, especially teacher education and distance language teaching and assessment, and learner corpora and mobile technologies for language learning.

Stavroula Tsiplakou is Associate Professor of linguistics and Academic Coordinator of the MA programme in Greek linguistics and literature. She holds a BA in Greek literature from the University of Athens, an M.Phil. in linguistics from the University of Cambridge and a PhD in Linguistics from the School of Oriental and African studies, University of London. Her research areas include syntax, pragmatics, text linguistics, sociolinguistics, and educational linguistics.

Foreword

Philip Hubbard[1]

We live in an era of constant change. Sometimes that change is moderate and steady, such as the growth of social media, online video, and smartphone apps over the past decade or so. At other times, the change is swift and dramatic, as we saw when much of the world suddenly had to shift from predominantly classroom teaching and learning, to predominantly online with the onset of COVID-19. This constant change is true of all fields, and language teaching is no exception. In order to keep up with this change, language teachers need to stay current with (1) developments in second language acquisition theory, research, and pedagogy, and (2) relevant technologies and applications for language learning both inside and outside the classroom. For language teacher educators, knowing how to stay up-to-date is even more important as they are responsible for preparing teacher candidates for a lifetime of teaching in an evolving and unpredictable future.

Language centers have an important role to play in achieving the aforementioned goals, supporting both teachers and teacher educators. They are often associated with specific institutions and thus draw on the teaching staff and students of their constituent foreign language programs or departments. In the US, where I come from, language centers can be independent units within a university or attached to a larger department, focused mainly on the needs of students at their institutions. However, there are also 16 national foreign language resource centers at universities around the country[2] that have an expanded role to provide materials and training beyond their institutional borders, each dedicated to a specific domain. For example, the *Center for Advanced Language Proficiency Education and Research* at Pennsylvania State University focuses on research and resources

---

1. Stanford University Language Center, Stanford, California, United States; phubbard@stanford.edu

2. https://www.nflrc.org/

How to cite: Hubbard, P. (2021). Foreword. In S. Papadima-Sophocleous, E. Kakoulli Constantinou & C. N. Giannikas (Eds), *Tertiary education language learning: a collection of research* (pp. xi-xv). Research-publishing.net. https://doi.org/10.14705/rpnet.2021.51.1250

Foreword

for developing language competence at the advanced level across all languages, while the *National African Language Resource Center* at the University of Indiana concentrates on the teaching and learning of African languages.

Despite the proliferation of language centers around the world, as the editors of the present work note, few publications specifically focus on the research produced by the faculty at a single language center. At one level, this absence is understandable – university hiring, promotion, and tenure committees tend to reward researchers whose work appears in highly-ranked peer-reviewed journals or in edited volumes from prestigious academic publishers. However, the present work demonstrates the potential of an alternative path, one that celebrates a collection of research papers from a single institution and supports its broad distribution to an audience of fellow practitioners.

The volume that follows represents the work of a group at the language center of one institution: the Cyprus University of Technology (CUT), collaboratively edited by three of its members. In doing so, it naturally provides an important resource for those who teach there and may be unaware of what their colleagues have discovered. However, by bringing this work to the level of a professional publication for wider distribution, the editors have also allowed those outside CUT the chance to learn from the research results of these chapter authors.

The editors' introduction does an excellent job of summarizing the content of the individual chapters and outlining common themes, and I do not intend to duplicate that here. Rather, I would like to say a few words about the language center from which these works sprang and then comment on several themes they mention.

According to its website, the CUT Language Center was founded in 2007 and focuses on three areas: language learning for specific purposes, Computer Assisted Language Learning (CALL), and teacher training in teaching Language for Specific Purposes (LSP). The vision statement for the language center contains ten points[3]: I believe three are particularly relevant here.

---

3. https://www.cut.ac.cy/faculties/languagecentre/the-department/

Philip Hubbard

- *To continuously develop as an internationally recognized Language Center with emphasis on innovation and linguistic diversity.* Innovation is the key word in this statement, and for innovation to be credible, it must be supported by empirical research demonstrating its effectiveness. The center is not just a consumer of research but a producer.

- *To offer knowledge and linguistic competence within the academic community.* The focus on offering knowledge to the academic community again is dependent on a strong and consistent research program, properly supported by the administration. Additionally, the production of works such as the present book allows for free dissemination of the center's contributions to colleagues.

- *To deliver the best possible culturally based second language education and training supported by the use of new technologies in order to foster high overall academic achievement in the choice of tertiary education options.* The commitment of the center to new technologies is reflected not only in many of the chapters in the present volume but also in its offering of a comprehensive online master's program in CALL linked to the Teaching English to Speakers of Other Languages (TESOL) technology standards.

It is relatively easy to come up with a set of vision statements like these, but the CUT Language Center turns these words into actions. There are indeed a number of faculty involved in research activities such as those underlying the chapters that follow, adding to the knowledge base of the field. The book is an admirable example of how useful research so often emerges from practice rather than being driven top-down by abstract theory. Thus, there is a pragmatism here that is missing from much of applied linguistics research, and I believe this makes the contributions more likely to impact teaching both inside and outside of CUT.

In their introduction, the editors note several themes, two of which are the teaching and learning of LSP and the role of new technologies. Readers

Foreword

interested in the former will find half of the papers concerned with that area. Of greater general interest, though, seven of the eight papers involve some form of technology mediation in the language learning process. The forms of this vary. In one course, the potential of CALL technologies in mediation processes is noted. In another, the use of assistive technologies to support students' memorization, concentration, and spelling is explored. Other papers illustrate the integration and impact of technology in developing critical thinking with multimodal texts, collaborative writing, online teacher education, virtual exchange, and embodied learning. The book thus offers a wealth of information regarding the affordances of various technologies for a range of applications in language learning and teacher training.

As mentioned previously, this book is special for its emerging solely from work within the CUT Language Center. However, it is worth noting that the three editors recently collaborated on two volumes related to teacher education. One was in the area of English for Specific Purposes (ESP): Papadima-Sophocleous, Kakoulli Constantinou, and Giannikas (2019), *ESP teaching and teacher education: current theories and practices*. The other, focused on technology, was with the Teacher Education Special Interest Group of EUROCALL: Giannikas, Kakoulli Constantinou, and Papadima-Sophocleous (2019), *Professional development in CALL: a selection of papers*. I encourage readers interested in teacher education to have a look at these works as well.

In addition to the three editors and the chapter authors, I would like to acknowledge the peer reviewers who gave freely of their time to providing the authors with valuable feedback: Fernando Loizides, Cardiff University; Elena Kkese, Cyprus University of Technology; Simone Torsani, Università degli Studi di Genova; Georgios Neokleous, Norwegian University of Science and Technology; David Barr, Ulster University; John Gillespie, Ulster University; Dimitra Karoulla-Vrikki, European University Cyprus; Stavroula Tsiplakou, Open University of Cyprus; Evangelia (Liana) Sakelliou, National and Kapodistrian University of Athens; Susanna Nocchi, Technological University Dublin; and Elisavet Kiourti, University of Nicosia and European University of Cyprus.

In closing, because of the rapidity with which technologies that mediate language learning and language use arise, it is more important than ever for language centers everywhere to become more involved not only in developing and maintaining the professional competence of their own teachers, but in sharing what they learn from the research in their particular contexts. I encourage readers to explore the chapters in the present volume to discover information of value for their own program administration, research, and teaching. Even more, I hope that *Tertiary education language learning: a collection of research* inspires faculty at other language centers to travel the same path, first producing useful research of their own and then disseminating it to interested colleagues around the world.

References

Giannikas, C. N., Kakoulli Constantinou, E., & Papadima-Sophocleous, S. (2019). (Eds). *Professional development in CALL: a selection of papers*. Research-publishing.net. https://doi.org/10.14705/rpnet.2019.28.9782490057283

Papadima-Sophocleous, S., Kakoulli Constantinou, E., & Giannikas, C. N. (2019). (Eds). *ESP teaching and teacher education: current theories and practices*. Research-publishing.net. https://doi.org/10.14705/rpnet.2019.33.9782490057450

Introduction

Salomi Papadima-Sophocleous[1], Elis Kakoulli Constantinou[2], and Christina Nicole Giannikas[3]

University language centres provide language-based courses to students of all disciplines. The principal *raison d'être* of a university language centre is to support any number of learner types, with a variety of reasons for learning a second or foreign language at tertiary level. These may include students and staff, external partners, and members of the public as part of a wider outreach strategy (Critchley, 2015). Language centres offer credit-bearing language courses and language enhancement programmes, general education, and service learning subjects. They also offer subjects for postgraduate research students and masters programmes. Qualities of pedagogic innovation, institutional adaptability, and effective use of technology have contributed to language centres' successful development (Ruane, 2003). Nonetheless, faculties of language centres offer more than their teaching, as many are involved in research activities. In agreement with Meyer (1997),

> "taking the concept of a Language Centre seriously means combining linguistic findings relevant to academic communication and its various genres with pedagogical insights derived from and applicable to the various categories of learners in an academic context, to form an integrated approach that treats the learners as candidates for or members of the international scientific community" (p. 11).

---

1. Cyprus University of Technology, Limassol, Cyprus; salomi.papadima@cut.ac.cy; https://orcid.org/0000-0003-4444-4482

2. Cyprus University of Technology, Limassol, Cyprus; elis.constantinou@cut.ac.cy; https://orcid.org/0000-0001-8854-3816

3. Cyprus University of Technology, Limassol, Cyprus; christina.giannikas@cut.ac.cy; https://orcid.org/0000-0002-5653-6803

How to cite: Papadima-Sophocleous, S., Kakoulli Constantinou, E., & Giannikas, C. N. (2021). Introduction. In S. Papadima-Sophocleous, E. Kakoulli Constantinou & C. N. Giannikas (Eds), *Tertiary education language learning: a collection of research* (pp. 1-6). Research-publishing.net. https://doi.org/10.14705/rpnet.2021.51.1251

Introduction

Despite the contributions language centres across the globe have made to language education and higher education in general, few publications have a specific focus on research work produced by language centre faculty.

The purpose of this edited volume, supported by the Cyprus University of Technology, is to fill some of this gap by focusing on the research activities of the faculty of a particular university language centre, that of the Cyprus University of Technology Language Centre, and displaying examples of research conducted in various fields of applied linguistics by its faculty members. The topics derive from their research interests and practice needs. A number of themes constitute the major aspects of most research. These include the teaching and learning of language for specific purposes, the role of new technologies in the enhancement of language learning, and the research emerging from their teaching practice which aims to improve teaching practices. Other research topics which are dealt with include mediation, multimodal texts, critical thinking, collaboration, Special Educational Needs (SEN), professional development, critical digital literacy, embodied learning, and classroom discourse.

The book focuses on the following:

- the potential of the Common European Framework of Reference (CEFR) for languages descriptors for mediation in an English for Specific Purposes (ESP) Computer Assisted Language Learning (CALL)-based context;

- multimodal texts in support of linguistic and critical thinking development in ESP;

- students' attitudes towards digital artefact creation through collaborative writing: the case of a Spanish for specific purposes class;

- the integration of assistive technologies in the SEN English for Academic Purposes (EAP) classroom: raising awareness;

- professional development in ESP: designing the curriculum of an online ESP teacher education course;

- technological mediation in a global competence virtual exchange project: a critical digital literacies perspective;

- the integration of embodied learning in a language learning classroom: conclusions from a qualitative analysis; and

- the pragmatic functions and the interpretations of the particle 'taha' (τάχα) in classroom discourse in the Cypriot-Greek dialect: the emergence of a new function.

More specifically, in chapter one **Maria Korai** and **Salomi Papadima-Sophocleous** examine the potential of the CEFR for languages descriptors for mediation, introduced in 2018, in an ESP (Rehabilitation Sciences) CALL-based CEFR B2 tertiary level context. Data collection tools included students' self-assessment against Can-do descriptors for mediation, observation, student reflections, and focus groups interviews. The findings suggest that the existing course activities had the potential to promote mediation processes. In addition, the CALL component of the ESP course activities highlighted the potential of CALL technologies to also trigger, support, and promote mediation processes.

In chapter two, **Stavroulla Hadjiconstantinou** explores how critical practices of identifying and negotiating the expression of personal opinion in multimodal texts, in an English for the media context particularly sensitive to issues of criticality, can enhance the development of multimodal literacy.

In chapter three, **María Victoria Soulé** analyses perceptions of technology-assisted collaborative writing, as well as collaborative writing processes in a Spanish for specific purposes class with students from the Department of Communication and Internet Studies. The analysis of the data revealed that the students' perceptions are mediated by task type, which in turn also affects collaborative writing patterns being the out-of-class activity, the one that presents a wider variety of writing styles as well as a more balanced participation among students.

In chapter four **Theodora Charalambous, Salomi Papadima-Sophocleous,** and **Christina Nicole Giannikas** present the case of the integration of assistive technologies in the SEN EAP classroom in an effort to raise awareness in the type of support given to university SEN EAP students with the use of Assistive Technologies (ATs) in SEN EAP contexts. Based on students' needs and analysis conducted by the instructor at the beginning of the course, the present study investigates the different ATs used by an SEN EAP instructor in order to support students' memorisation, concentration, and spelling. Furthermore, it investigates the SEN EAP students' attitudes towards the specialised EAP process.

Chapter five presents the work of **Elis Kakoulli Constantinou** and **Salomi Papadima-Sophocleous** who discuss their findings on professional development in ESP. The chapter describes the development of a curriculum for an online ESP Teacher Education (TE) course, the ReTEESP Online. The course was based on a literature review in ESP and ESP TE, including learning theories and TE models, and recent developments in curriculum design. The course was also informed by an analysis of the 24 language instructors' needs in ESP TE and a pilot implementation of the course.

In chapter six, **Anna Nicolaou** discusses technological mediation in a global competence virtual exchange project, from a critical digital literacies perspective. The study explores the students' perceptions about digital skills development through their participation in a global competence virtual exchange project. It also examines the ways in which students interact with technology in order to develop global competence and active citizenship.

In chapter seven, **Panagiotis Kosmas** explores the integration of embodied learning in a language learning classroom. The study examines whether this practice would improve students' language performance and enhance their engagement in, and motivation for, learning a language. Elementary students and teachers were involved in the study and data were collected from video recordings of intervention sessions in the classroom. The results reveal that the embodied learning practice enabled students to actively engage in the lesson, increasing their motivation and participation. The use of such an embodied learning approach in language learning and teaching is discussed.

The book closes with chapter eight, where **Fotini Efthimiou** examines the pragmatic functions, the meanings and the interpretations of 'taha' (τάχα) in classroom discourse in the Greek-Cypriot dialect. Data from a three hour recording of the participants' speech were collected and analysed, and 32 critical episodes that included 'taha' were isolated. Students were also asked to note the function of 'taha' through the use of a questionnaire, and to interpret its functions through a discussion. Following the pragmatic analysis proposed by Tsiplakou and Papapetrou (2020), the current research concluded that the basic meaning of 'taha' ('supposedly'/'allegedly') may perform several pragmatic functions, depending on the context.

The eight chapters of the volume *Tertiary education language learning* showcase the type of research conducted at a university language centre. It showcases some common themes as well as some specific research interests in varied areas of applied linguistics. The examples indicate that research in contexts, such as the specific language centre, draws from the needs of these contexts and strives to solve problems.

It is expected that this volume will appeal to university language centre practitioners, and provide insights in current research conducted in university language centres. The volume will also attract the interest of other educational institution practitioners who would be interested in similar topics. Moreover, the volume may also be useful to language researchers, teacher trainers, practitioners, policymakers, material developers, university curriculum academic bodies, as well as any other language education specialists who may be interested in what is happening in language centres. The editors hope that the present contribution will be viewed as a valuable addition to the literature and a worthy scholarly achievement.

Acknowledgements

The editors of *Tertiary education language learning: a collection of research* would like to wholeheartedly thank the Cyprus University of Technology, the financial support of which made the publication of this volume possible.

References

Critchley, M. (2015). *The role of language centres in higher education*. https://www.dur.ac.uk/cfls/about/role/

Meyer, H. J. (1997). Language centres and the international dimension of university life. In D. Little & B. Voss (Eds), *Language centres: planning for the new millennium* (pp. 3-12). CercleS.

Ruane, M. (2003). Language centres in higher education: facing the challenge. *ASp, 41-42*, 5-20. https://doi.org/10.4000/asp.1127

Tsiplakou, S., & Papapetrou, C. (2020). *Two dialects, one particle—taha?* [white paper]. https://www.academia.edu/43265788/Two_dialects_one_particle_taha

1. The potential of the CEFR for languages descriptors for mediation in an ESP CALL-based context

Maria Korai[1] and Salomi Papadima-Sophocleous[2]

Abstract

The present case study investigated the potential of the Common European Framework of Reference (CEFR) for languages: learning, teaching, assessment can-do descriptors for mediation in an English for Specific Purposes (ESP) Computer-Assisted Language Learning (CALL)-based context. Fabricating descriptors for mediation was cardinal for the Council of Europe's (2018) endeavour in updating the CEFR Companion. Despite surfacing just as a language skill in the 2001 CEFR Companion, mediation is now viewed as a central mode of communication in the New CEFR Companion, both in the receptive and productive modes. As they were just introduced in 2018, the CEFR mediation descriptor scales have not yet been sufficiently explored. The main goal of the present research was to fill some of this gap in the literature by investigating the potential of the CEFR for languages descriptors for mediation in an ESP CALL-based CEFR B2 tertiary level context (a 13 week ESP course specifically designed to meet the needs of university Rehabilitation Sciences students.) Data collection tools included students' self-assessment against can-do descriptors for mediation, observation, student reflections, and focus group interviews. The findings suggest that the implementation of the existing course activities had the potential to promote mediation processes. The significant role of mediation in carrying out the course

1. Cyprus University of Technology, Limassol, Cyprus; mariakorai3@gmail.com; https://orcid.org/0000-0002-3406-0154

2. Cyprus University of Technology, Limassol, Cyprus; salomi.papadima@cut.ac.cy; https://orcid.org/0000-0003-4444-4482

How to cite: Korai, M., & Papadima-Sophocleous, S. (2021). The potential of the CEFR for languages descriptors for mediation in an ESP CALL-based context. In S. Papadima-Sophocleous, E. Kakoulli Constantinou & C. N. Giannikas (Eds), *Tertiary education language learning: a collection of research* (pp. 7-28). Research-publishing.net. https://doi.org/10.14705/rpnet.2021.51.1252

Chapter 1

activities in addition to the CALL component of the ESP course activities highlighted the potential of CALL technologies to trigger, support, and promote mediation processes; this finding stressed the underlying role of the nature and the structure of the ESP course's CALL-Based activities in supporting mediation processes.

Keywords: common European framework of reference, mediation descriptors, English for specific purposes, computer-assisted language learning.

1. Introduction

The present case study focuses on the potential of the CEFR for languages: learning, teaching, assessment can-do descriptors for mediation in an ESP CALL-based context. The fabrication and validation of the descriptors for mediation originated from the Council of Europe's painstaking work on language learning, assessment, and teaching. While it was originally treated as a language skill in the 2001 CEFR Companion, mediation is reinterpreted and viewed as one of the basic ingredients in communication in the New CEFR Companion. The emergence of mediation as a language skill in the 2001 CEFR Companion was perhaps the preamble to the reinterpretation of mediation in the New CEFR Companion.

In the updated New CEFR Companion, mediation is treated as a fundamental mode of communication; not only the significance of the co-construction of meaning but also "the constant movement between the individual and social level in language learning" (Council of, Europe, 2018, p. 9) led to the development of descriptor scales for mediation from scratch. As they were just introduced in 2018, the CEFR mediation descriptor scales were still underexplored at the moment this research was conducted. The present research aspired to fill some of this gap in the literature by providing insights regarding the potential of the CEFR descriptors for mediation, not just in a general English learning context but in an ESP CALL-based context.

2. Literature review

Commencing with an overview of the CEFR, its definition and background, this chapter describes and discusses the CEFR descriptive scheme as well as the theoretical components of the present inquiry.

2.1. The CEFR: definition and background

The CEFR is a ground-breaking product of the Council of Europe's work on language teaching and learning. It was originated in the 1970s by the "need for a common framework for language learning which would "facilitate cooperation among educational institutions in different countries", particularly within Europe (Council of Europe, 2001, p. 5). It was officially published in 2001 and it is available in 40 languages.

The CEFR presents a comprehensive descriptive scheme of language proficiency and a set of common reference levels (A1-C2) defined in illustrative descriptor scales. Investing in socio-cultural and social constructivist approaches, the CEFR envisions and builds upon the idea of learners as social agents who co-construct meaning in interaction and by the notions of mediation and plurilingual/ pluricultural competences (Council of Europe, 2018, p. 24). As an advocate of social constructivism, the CEFR assumes an action-oriented approach; it proposes real-life tasks for the learners, which involve the use of language as a vehicle to accomplish the tasks of different natures at an individual, as well as at a peer/group, level.

2.2. The CEFR descriptive scheme

The CEFR descriptive scheme is "not in [itself] offered as standard" but it is "intended to provide a common metalanguage to facilitate networking and the development of communities of practice by groups of teachers" (Council of Europe, 2018, pp. 41-42). It can be used as a point of reference to analyse L2 learners' needs, identify their learning goals, and drive the development of L2 curriculum (Little, 2006).

Chapter 1

The CEFR framework of levels describes language proficiency and is part of the Council of Europe's endeavour to promote plurilingualism and pluriculturalism among the countries of Europe (Council of Europe, 2018). The framework of levels is divided into three parts: the *global stage (A1-C2)*; the *CEFR self-assessment grid*, which is presented in the form of checklists; and the *illustrative descriptor scales for the activities*.

The CEFR levels organise 'can-do' statements, the formation of which was inspired by the field of professional training for nurses (Council of Europe, 2018, p. 32). The can-do statements are concerned with the learner's communicative language competences and the strategies that are intertwined with these competences, as well as communicative activities. Communicative language activities revolve around reception, production, interaction, and mediation. Likewise, there are scales for listening and reading, speaking, and writing.

2.3. Implementation of the CEFR in language learning

Working with the CEFR in language learning settings has received the interest of a plethora of researchers and in-service practitioners (Alderson et al., 2006; Glover, 2011; Goodier, 2014; Harsch & Rupp, 2011; Lowie, Haines, & Jansma, 2010; Weir, 2005). The following are some examples of research in different areas.

Harsch and Rupp's (2011) study uses the CEFR as a basis to design level-specific writing tasks. Adopting a descriptive statistics analysis combined with generalisability and multifaceted Rasch modelling, Harsch and Rupp (2011) conclude that the level-specific writing tasks "yield plausible inferences about task difficulty, rater harshness, rating criteria difficulty, and student distribution" (p. 28); as a result they can be aligned to their targeted CEFR levels.

In a similar fashion, Glover (2011) adopts a mixed methods approach to examine the potential of the CEFR level descriptors in raising university students' awareness of their speaking skills; throughout the study, positive findings were reported such as the potential of the CEFR descriptors for self-assessment to promote active involvement in learning and reflection, "resulting in greater self-awareness and a more realistic view of the learners' own abilities" (p. 130).

Weir (2005) views can-do statements from the assessment and testing perspective; while he highlights the potential of the can-do statements, Weir (2005) also points out their major limitation; as Weir (2005) posits, "the can-do statements can be successfully performed at each level of proficiency even if their wording is not consistent or not transparent enough in places for the development of tests" (p. 282). The density of the CEFR descriptors is discussed by Goodier (2014) too; he views it as one of the CEFR weakest points. In *Working with the CEFR can-do statements,* Goodier (2014) reveals the difficulty of the participants in his study to understand the CEFR descriptors, as they thought they were "dense and wordy" (p. 26).

Focusing on the assessment of writing tasks, Lowie et al. (2010) have conducted a case study of embedding a standardisation procedure within the CEFR framework at the University of Groningen; throughout their study, positive results were reported highlighting the value of standardisation procedures within the CEFR. Along the same lines, Alderson et al. (2006) view the CEFR in relation to the analysis of tests of reading and listening through the experience of the Dutch CEFR Construct project. The method used in the project was "iterative and inductive" (Alderson et al., 2006, p. 7). Based on their findings, Alderson et al. (2006) conclude that, despite being promising as an instrument for developing tests, the CEFR needed "additional specifications to be developed before [it] could be used as the basis for test development" (p. 6).

Identifying reported problems can lead to the revision and amendment of the CEFR by the stakeholders (Trim, 2012). This is precisely exemplified through the publication of the 2018 *CEFR Companion Volume with New Descriptors*. In the 2018 CEFR Companion, readers are introduced to the illustrative descriptors for mediation alongside with the notions of plurilingual and pluricultural competences. Descriptor scales are also provided for sign languages and young language learners.

Chapter 1

The present research sought to unravel the potential of the can-do statements for mediation in an ESP CALL-based university classroom.

2.4. Mediation

The concept of mediation is echoed in Vygotsky's (1934) theory of constructivism. It involves "the use of culturally-derived psychological tools in transforming the relations between psychological inputs and outputs" (Vygotsky, 1934, p. 3). Vygotsky's (1934) theory of constructivism embraces the idea that humans do not act directly in the world but rather the use of mediation aids in altering their understanding through interacting with others and their environment. Mediation can also involve the use of symbolic tools within a socially organised activity. Language can function as a symbolic tool used by humans to mediate their relationship to their environment and to others. Vygotsky (1934) coined the term Zone of Proximal Development (ZPD), which is founded upon the co-construction of meaning and could be defined as the rupture between someone's actual competence and their individual prospective development level.

2.5. The CEFR and mediation

Espousing the premises of Vygotsky (1934), the CEFR builds upon the concept of mediation. While it has initially surfaced in the CEFR since 2001 (Council of Europe, 2001), mediation has tended to be reduced to interpretation and translation (Council of Europe, 2001). In the CEFR New Companion, 'mediation' is an all embracing nomadic notion (Lenoir, 1996) since it is one of the basic ingredients in communication, both in the receptive and productive modes.

Mediation lies at the heart of the CEFR's aforementioned vision; hence the concept is viewed from different angles in the New CEFR Companion. Commencing with the classification of mediation into four fundamental types being linguistic, cultural, social, and pedagogic (Council of Europe, 2018), mediation is further categorised in two forms that are essentially employed with the use of language: cognitive mediation and relational mediation. Cognitive mediation can be defined as the facilitation of access to knowledge in cases where a person cannot access it by himself/herself, whereas relational mediation can be thought of as the effective management of interpersonal relations, which aims in the creation of collaborative environments. Based on the two aforementioned forms of mediation, the authors of the CEFR split mediation into four subgroups (see figure in Council of Europe, 2018, p. 104).

2.6. ESP

ESP is defined as a "discipline that attempts to meet the needs of a specific population of students, employs methodologies and materials from the discipline it is centred on, and focuses on the discourse related to it" (Dudley-Evans & St John, 1998, p. 5). ESP can be linked with special academic and professional areas that take an approach to language teaching which has as a main purpose, that purpose is to fulfil the specific needs of the learners engaged with it. Curriculum design and syllabus construction should be relevant to the needs of the ESP students. Instead of 'one fits all' approach, demarcating genre analysis is central to ESP. Needs analysis is equally important to ESP courses; Athanasiou et al. (2016), postulate that "needs analysis refers to the process through which the language and skills that the learners need are identified" (p. 300). By the same token, being exposed to authentic material is beneficial for the ESP students as it prepares them for different target situations.

2.7. CALL

CALL debuted in early 1960 and it refers to "the search for and study of applications of the computer in language teaching and learning" (Levy & Stockwell, 1997, p. 1). CALL can inform any language learning context as it is "very flexible and can adapt to the facilitator's teaching philosophy and learning objectives" (Ducate & Arnold, 2011, p. 9); in the present case study, the existing ESP course was framed within the CALL field.

With the proliferation of technologies that support language learning such as Web 2.0 tools and virtual learning environments, as well as the different approaches to teaching and learning, the 21st century CALL is at the service of the urge to prepare learners who will not only be competent language learners but also competent digital natives. In a CALL context, integrating pedagogically driven technologies is a cardinal principle. The use of authentic materials and the provision of real-world problems are also CALL components; dealing with real-world problems in a meaningful way encourages students to become active learners and critically engage with information using technology as the vehicle for constructing their learning. In light of the aforementioned, it is reasonable to argue that mediation is at the core of CALL; in a CALL context, technology precisely mediates language learning and use as, not only learners become users of the language, but also technology becomes the mediator of the learners' language use (Stanford University, 2020).

2.8. CEFR, ESP, and CALL

Within the ESP research agenda, only a limited amount of studies deals with the CEFR and ESP. Mestre and Pastor (2013), for example, adopt a mixed methods approach to explore the pragmatic considerations of the CEFR within an ESP context; Mestre and Pastor (2013) report positive results "as students acquired information about pragmatic aspects of language" (p. 229). A quite different approach is taken by Athanasiou et al. (2016); using focus groups, Athanasiou et al. (2016) discuss the process of alignment of ESP courses with the CEFR in the Cyprus University of Technology. According to Athanasiou et al. (2016), while the ESP syllabus requires expertise in terms of the discourse related to each course, the selection of material is a painstaking process which is further aggravated with its alignment with a specific language level. In a similar fashion, Grytsyk (2016) explores the positive outcomes of the CEFR in the ESP curriculum in Ukrainian higher educational institutions, obtaining favourable results; as she states, "[t]he implementation of International English Tests into the process of teaching ESP in accordance with CEFR will undoubtedly lead to positive changes and transformations of the foreign language education" (Grytsyk, 2016, p. 8). Buyukkalay (2017) approaches the CEFR from a different angle in her study; the author examines the effect of CEFR-based ESP speaking and listening activities on the success of students in the Faculty of Tourism, reporting an increase in the achievement levels of the students in the aforementioned skills.

2.9. Literature review conclusive remarks

Despite the published research findings in relation to the CEFR and ESP, however, so far little is known about the descriptors for mediation in language learning contexts, let alone in ESP CALL-based language learning contexts. A notable effort to deal with mediation in language teaching is made by Chovancová (2018) who draws attention to the centrality of mediation in the context of English for Legal Purposes (ELP) and ESP; in her article *Practicing the skill of mediation in English for legal purposes*, the researcher discusses the potential of mediation for effective teaching of ESP focusing on ELP. Chovancová (2018) primarily designs sample activities to gain an understanding regarding the application of mediation in the context of legal practice and the English for law syllabus. She then suggests ways in which students can practise the skill of mediation. Regardless of the fertile ground for practising the skill of mediation in an ESP/ELP classroom provided by Chovancová's (2018) research, actual implementation of the aforementioned in ESP contexts, as well as in ESP CALL-based contexts, needs to be staged too. In this way, the CEFR stakeholders can be further illuminated regarding the harmonisation of the theoretical part of mediation developed in the companion, and the practical one in language learning contexts.

3. Method

In the field of applied linguistics, there is a plethora of research approaches and research designs. Scholars opt for the one that best serves their research. The nature of the present inquiry fulfilled the premises of a case study research design and mixed research method. The present study was an empirical inquiry that investigated the recent contemporary phenomenon of the CEFR Descriptors for mediation in depth and within a real-world context (Yin, 2014, p. 4), that of an ESP CALL-based language learning. Exploring the potential of the descriptors for mediation in this specific context provided valuable insights regarding their utility not in general English language learning context, but in a specific one. More strikingly, by carrying out the study within not just an ESP context but rather within an ESP CALL-based context, amplified the significance of the present inquiry as it also helped to gain insights into the potential of technology in triggering, supporting, or promoting mediation processes. A mixed research method was employed. Data were collected using observation, learner self-assessment against can-do statements for mediation, learner reflections, and focus group interviews. It addressed the following questions.

- How is mediation present in the existing ESP curriculum of this case study?

- How do the ESP CALL-based course activities of this case study support mediation?

3.1. ESP CALL-based context and participants

The study was conducted in an ESP CALL-based CEFR B2 level language classroom at a tertiary level context. The course lasted for 13 weeks. Students attended the course twice a week in two one and a half hour-long sessions. The course was specifically designed to meet the needs of university Rehabilitation Sciences. Through the course, students were afforded the opportunity to develop language competencies in English that would allow them to attain their professional goals as qualified speech therapists. The course was also framed within the CALL field; hence students performed independent or collaborative task-based activities (in fixed groups of three or four) using technology; they actively participated in interactive lectures and activities; and they developed their skills in all areas of language learning through the use of authentic material and content related to the genres and topics of the field of Rehabilitation Sciences, revolving around four main thematic areas:

- clinical aspects in the autism spectrum disorders (Thematic area/ Block 4);

- the elderly and rehabilitation, hearing rehabilitation, stroke rehabilitation (Thematic area/Block 5);

- an introduction to the principles of rehabilitation based on the international classification of functioning, disability, and health framework; and

- head injury rehabilitation, spinal injury rehabilitation.

This compulsory course was offered by the University Language Centre to first-year Rehabilitation Sciences students. Twelve first-year Greek Cypriot university participants enrolled in this English for specific academic purposes course of the language centre were recruited for volunteer participation in the case study.

3.2. Process

The research adopted a design plan for organising the stages of carrying out the study and thus ensuring the smooth transition from one stage to another.

The first stage of the implementation plan dealt with the adaptation by the researcher of the CEFR generic descriptors for mediation to the two existing ESP thematic blocks within the study's timeframe. This included the adaptation of the descriptors to the ESP course activities: oral discussion of lectures, note taking, summary writing of lectures, interview preparation and conduct of the interview, critical thinking, critical analysis, and collaborative writing of an article.

The second stage revolved around obtaining consent, familiarising students with the CEFR and the CEFR framework for mediation, and administering to students the adapted CEFR descriptors to the first ESP block.

The third stage was dedicated to observing the implementation of Block 4's course activities, re-administrating the adapted CEFR descriptors for mediation to ESP Block 4, providing participants with the template for reflections on

Block 4, and administering to students the adapted CEFR descriptors for mediation to ESP Block 5.

Likewise, the fourth stage was devoted to observing the implementation of Block 5's course activities, re-administrating the adapted CEFR descriptors for mediation to ESP Block 5, and providing participants with the template for reflections on Block 5.

The fifth stage focused on focus group interviews for exploring the participants' perceptions of the nature and implementation of the descriptors for mediation through their course activities.

The final stage of carrying out the project dealt with data analysis, discussion of findings, and conclusions.

3.3. Research design, method, and data collection tools

The present research study made use of both qualitative and quantitative evidence, in other words, it followed the quantitative/qualitative mixed methods research process (Creswell & Plano Clark, 2011). Quantitative data were collected from the administration of the CEFR self-assessment can-do statements for mediation before and after the implementation of the existing ESP course activities. Qualitative data were collected from the researcher's observations and the focus group's interviews. Qualitative data were also collected from the students' reflections for further validation of the results.

Each of the thematic blocks' tasks was classified under the appropriate mediation descriptor and a total of 61 items were created. The adapted CEFR table was administered to the students both before and after the implementation of the existing ESP course activities. Participants were asked to indicate on the adapted CEFR descriptor scales for mediation what they can-do with language in processes that entailed mediation; in particular, they were asked to rate their ability to execute the tasks described in each statement on a scale ranging from A1 to B2.

Observation. Using the adapted CEFR descriptor scales for mediation as an observational protocol, the researchers collected data by making a field visit to the case study site, which was the ESP language classroom. The observations involved participants' behaviours and interactions in relation to their course activities and the descriptors for mediation during course sessions of two thematic blocks.

Student reflections. Aided by a set of guiding questions formulated by the researchers, students were invited by the end of each thematic block to reflect on their learning in relation to the mediation processes involved.

Focus groups. Focus group interviewing was also used for exploring the participants' perceptions of the nature and implementation of the descriptors for mediation through their course activities. The focus group interview was conducted in the participants' L1 and it was implemented in two identical group sessions, whereby the participants were split into two groups and they responded to identical questions.

4. Results and discussion

The main goal of the present research was to fill some of the gap in the literature regarding the potential of the CEFR mediation descriptor scales in an ESP (Rehabilitation Sciences) CALL-based CEFR B2 tertiary level context. The results and their discussion are presented below by answering the research questions:

4.1. Question 1: how is mediation present in the existing ESP curriculum of this case study?

Primarily, the adaptation of the CEFR descriptors for mediation to the existing ESP curriculum revealed high prevalence of mediation in the ESP curriculum despite the designers' unawareness of the CEFR framework for mediation before this study. Investing in observations, the researchers confirmed that mediation was indeed systematically present in the implemented ESP curriculum, although the curriculum designers did not originally take it into consideration as their course was developed just before the CEFR descriptors for mediation were published in 2018.

The presence of mediation in the course activities was reflected in both the structure and the content of the course in a systematic way. Not only could students mediate to themselves through reading and responding critically to texts, but they could also use technologies to work collaboratively on authentic tasks related to their field of study. The tasks were arranged according to the degree of the difficulty needed for their accomplishment; note taking, oral discussion, summary writing, interview preparation, conduct of the interview, critical analysis. By the same token, the authentic nature of the topics related to the participants' field of study, as well as the use of CALL technologies in performing the tasks, encouraged mediation processes in a meaningful way. More strikingly, the instructor's guidance and support to the performance of the tasks included mediation processes, such as the simplification of her language to explain concepts regarding the course content.

The identification of the high prevalence of mediation in the ESP curriculum was directly linked to the second research question which referred to how the ESP course activities of this case study supported mediation.

4.2. Question 2: how do the ESP CALL-based course activities of this case study support mediation?

By employing the concurrent embedded strategy, we were able to explore the potential of the ESP course activities to support mediation, both in general and in particular. Through the primary method we quantitatively explored the potential of the ESP course activities in enhancing the skill of mediation. Through the secondary method we identified which activities were more conducive to mediation processes and what the specific mediation processes entailed in performing them were.

Table 1. Results of participants' self-assessment against can-do statements for mediation before the implementation of the CEFR descriptors for mediation

BEFORE					
B1		**A2**		**A1**	
Mean	2.409836066	Mean	7.06557377	Mean	2.557377049
Standard Error	0.208267704	Standard Error	0.348195075	Standard Error	0.311461029
Median	2	Median	7	Median	2
Mode	2	Mode	6	Mode	0
Standard Deviation	1.626622771	Standard Deviation	2.71949047	Standard Deviation	2.432588403
Sample Variance	2.645901639	Sample Variance	7.395628415	Sample Variance	5.917486339
Kurtosis	0.178994903	Kurtosis	-0.851587225	Kurtosis	-1.021219129
Skewness	0.526938003	Skewness	-0.163908437	Skewness	0.524016906
Range	7	Range	11	Range	8
Minimum	0	Minimum	1	Minimum	0
Maximum	7	Maximum	12	Maximum	8
Sum	147	Sum	431	Sum	156
Count	61	Count	61	Count	61

Table 2. Results of participants' self-assessment against can-do statements for mediation after the implementation of the CEFR descriptors for mediation

AFTER					
B1		**A2**		**A1**	
Mean	5.06557377	Mean	6.147540984	Mean	0.786885246
Standard Error	0.177826668	Standard Error	0.185301505	Standard Error	0.090881398
Median	5	Median	6	Median	1
Mode	5	Mode	6	Mode	1
Standard Deviation	1.388870674	Standard Deviation	1.447251021	Standard Deviation	0.709806408
Sample Variance	1.928961749	Sample Variance	2.094535519	Sample Variance	0.503825137
Kurtosis	0.190633255	Kurtosis	-0.263933396	Kurtosis	-0.940383748
Skewness	0.612414235	Skewness	-0.36847889	Skewness	0.333315645

Chapter 1

Range	6	Range	6	Range	2
Minimum	3	Minimum	3	Minimum	0
Maximum	9	Maximum	9	Maximum	2
Sum	309	Sum	375	Sum	48
Count	61	Count	61	Count	61

Data analysis of students' self-assessment against the can-do statements for mediation included descriptive statistics analysis to quantitatively describe the collection of information regarding students' self-assessment before and after the implementation of the existing ESP course activities. Results of students' self-assessment against the adapted CEFR can-do statements for mediation to the two existing ESP thematic blocks' activities before and after the implementation of the existing ESP course activities are presented in Table 1 and Table 2 above.

Overall, quantitative data analysis of the 61 CEFR can-do statements for self-assessment revealed development of students' skills for mediation after the implementation of the ESP CALL-based course activities, including mediation. While the mean value of the A2 and A1 proficiency levels, for example, decreased after the implementation of the ESP course activities, the mean value of the B1 proficiency level increased. By the same token, the total number of A2 statements was declined after the implementation of the existing ESP course activities (from 431 to 375), indicating that a number of students rated themselves as B1; in addition to the aforementioned, the dramatic decline of A1 statements limits the possibility of students self-assessment as A1. This is supported by the subtraction of the total number of A2 statements noted within the two phases of the administration of the adapted can-do descriptors for mediation, which is bigger than the total number of A1 statements. These findings had positive implications in that they suggested the potential of the ESP course activities in enhancing the skill of mediation; in performing and accomplishing the ESP course tasks, students considered that they could develop their communicative skills regarding the mode of mediation.

Qualitative data analysis from observation, student reflections, and focus group interview confirmed that the course activities were valuable from the angle of mediation. The data revealed that mediation processes were greatly employed in the course activities; however, mediation seemed to be more conspicuously employed in the course writing activities and the collaborative oral discussions rather than the oral classroom discussions. Data analysis also revealed the significance of the CALL component of the ESP course activities from the angle of mediation as the technologies used by the students for performing their tasks were demonstrated to spark, support, and promote mediation practices too.

Mediation processes were thoroughly manifested in note taking, summary writing, preparation for questions and answers for an interview, and critical analysis for an article. Note taking was an individual task and it was mostly used by the students as a method for drawing attention to the main points of the lecture; organising their notes in bullet points according to the subtitles of their lectures and then expanding on them by including examples entails a form of mediation as students related in writing specific information contained in their lectures, and they made sense of it by structuring their notes in a clear way (Council of Europe, 2018, pp. 108, 115). The use of Google Docs for note taking enabled students' exchange of their notes with their peers and it facilitated the process of the collaborative tasks: lectures' summaries, questions and answers for an interview, and critical analysis of an article. While one of the students stated that "[n]ote-taking helped me to understand the lecture and it provided the basis for composing the summary", another student maintained: "I consider that note taking aided me in understanding the content of the lecture and it helped me to pay attention to the speaker's details which were the main points".

Notably, in collaborative writing activities, there was a distribution of the tasks to be performed by each group member with specific people assuming the role of leaders and the rest of the group members taking on an assisting and supporting role. Participants acting as leaders (CEFR: mediating concepts/leading group work) not only led group work but they also encouraged their peers' contribution to the task (CEFR: mediating concepts/encouraging conceptual talk). As a result, they facilitated communication within their group; while they opened the group discussion on the tasks by proposing their arguments, they provided explanations to their peers regarding the content and the nature of the task. In providing explanations to their peers, the participants/leaders were sometimes observed to switch to their classmates' mother tongue so as to help them to capture complex vocabulary such as 'rehabilitation' and 'face transplants'. The participants/leaders' scaffolding practices towards their peers emphasised mediation strategies surfacing in collaborative tasks; breaking down complicated information contained in the written or spoken texts from the lecture and the articles, or adapting language to explain to their peers, are classified under *Mediation strategies* in the CEFR framework for mediation (Council of Europe, 2018, p. 104). Eventually, aided by the participants/leaders, the rest of the group members made their contributions to the summary composition, the preparation of the interview questions and answers, and the critical analysis tasks; the participants/assistants' contributions included simple remarks regarding the content of the tasks as well as the selection of the vocabulary to be included in crafting the written documents. Students themselves acknowledged the importance of collaboration in accomplishing the tasks as exemplified through their assertive tone and their perception of it in the following statements.

> "Collaborative work is better than individual work because in this way there are different viewpoints and you can learn from each other" (P2).

> "In collaborative tasks, one complements the other and this is useful as it allows for accomplishing the task more successfully" (P10).

> "If a person didn't understand something the rest of the group members can help him/her and then s/he can contribute to the task" (P5).

Mediation practices were likewise fairly exploited through the oral discussion; mediation practices from the oral discussion mostly revolved around clarification requests regarding the content and the relevant terminology of the lecture or the guidelines for performing a task. This is exemplified through the following interactions:

> "Can you please explain to me the definition of diagnosis?" (P8).

"Does anyone know what a diagnosis is?" (Instructor)

"Diagnosis is to come to a conclusion of what the problem is" (P6).

"Do we have to be neutral in descriptive writing and negative or positive in critical writing?" (P5).

"Critical writing entails providing arguments and then distancing oneself from them to criticise them by using evidence from reliable sources" (Instructor).

Not only through the above and similar interactions did students employed mediation processes, but they also noted in their self-reports that the oral discussion of the lecture was helpful as it allowed them to clarify their thoughts and it facilitated their understanding of the lecture content.

By contrast, the participants did not systematically express their personal responses to the oral discussions carried out in the classroom, although they were encouraged by their instructor to engage with them. The pattern of low participation in terms of expressing a personal response to the oral discussions, nevertheless, could be linked to personality traits or to the lack of insufficient prior practice in the oral discussion, rather than implying the absence of mediation practices.

Having direct access to CALL technologies for performing the existing ESP course tasks enhanced students' mediation practices. Watching preselected instructional YouTube videos contributed to students' understanding of the course topics and the preliminary processes in performing them. For example, once students watched the YouTube video about 'strokes', they seemed to gain a better understanding of the task to be performed – the preparation of questions and answers for an interview. Upon watching the video, students were illuminated about the aforementioned topic as well as about the kind of questions and answers that describe an interview, and eventually they worked on their assigned topic accordingly (Autism/SLI/ADD/ADHD/Genetic Syndromes).

Moreover, the projection of the presentation on the classroom board aided students in presenting their ideas to the rest of the groups and also scaffolded them in understanding the components of the topic addressed. Likewise, the use of Google Docs for the writing tasks was demonstrated as a valuable venue to construct knowledge; through the simultaneous input of information and the alterations and additions of each other's written productions, students could not only collaborate with each other but they could also negotiate for meaning and consolidate their knowledge.

4.3. Limitations

One may argue that the results of a case study do not allow for generalisation. However, the aim of a case study is not generalisation, it is the in-depth examination of a case. In this case, it is the in-depth inquiry of the integration of the CEFR descriptors for mediation, not in general, but in the specific case of ESP CALL-based context. The focus was to shed light on the details of this integration and aid in the understanding of the underlying reasons that establish them as favourable beyond the site of the specific context.

5. Conclusions

The in-depth analysis of the introduction of the CEFR can-do descriptors for mediation in the ESP context revealed issues that have not yet been exposed in prior research, and provided important implications for practice. The case study revealed that not only was mediation systematically present in the existing ESP curriculum, but also that the implementation of the existing ESP course activities had the potential to promote mediation processes. The significant role of mediation in carrying out the course activities, in addition to the CALL component of the ESP CALL-based course activities, highlighted the potential of CALL technologies in triggering, supporting, and promoting mediation processes; this finding places emphasis on the underlying role of the nature and the structure of the ESP course activities in supporting mediation processes.

6. Acknowledgements

We would like to thank the Rehabilitation Sciences students and instructors, for making this research possible.

References

Alderson, J. C., Figueras, N., Kuijper, H., Nold, G., Takala, S., & Tardieu, C. (2006). Analysing tests of reading and listening in relation to the common European framework of reference: the experience of the Dutch CEFR construct project. *Language Assessment Quarterly*, *3*(1), 3-30. https://doi.org/10.1207/s15434311laq0301_2

Athanasiou, A., Constantinou, E. K., Neophytou, M., Nicolaou, A., Sophocleous, S. P., & Yerou, C. (2016). Aligning ESP courses with the common European framework of reference for languages. *Language Learning in Higher Education*, *6*(2), 297-316.

Buyukkalay, N. (2017). *The effects of CEFR-based ESP speaking and listening activities: the effects of CEFR-based ESP speaking and listening activities on the success of students in faculties of tourism*. Lambert Academic Publishing.

Chovancová, B. (2018). Practicing the skill of mediation in English for legal purposes. *Studies in Logic, Grammar and Rhetoric*, *53*(1), 49-60. https://doi.org/10.2478/slgr-2018-0003

Council of Europe. (2001). *Common European Framework of Reference for Languages: learning, teaching, assessment*. Cambridge University Press.

Council of Europe. (2018). *CEFR companion volume with new descriptors*.

Creswell, J. W., & Plano Clark, V. L. (2011). Choosing a mixed methods design. *Designing and conducting mixed methods research*, *2*, 53-106.

Ducate, L., & Arnold, N. (2011). Technology, CALL, and the net generation: where are we headed from here?. In L. Ducate & N. Arnold (Eds), *Present and future promises of CALL: from theory and research to new directions in language teaching* (pp. 1-22). CALICO.

Dudley-Evans, T., & St John, M. J. (1998). *Developments in English for specific purposes: a multi-disciplinary approach*. Cambridge University Press.

Glover, P. (2011). Using CEFR level descriptors to raise university students' awareness of their speaking skills. *Language Awareness*, *20*(2), 121-133. https://doi.org/10.1080/09658416.2011.555556

Goodier, T. (2014). *Working with CEFR can-do statements: an investigation of UK English language teacher beliefs and published materials*. Unpublished MA dissertation. King's College.

Grytsyk, N. (2016). Implementing European standards in the ESP curriculum for students of non-linguistic specialities in Ukrainian universities. *Advanced Education*. https://doi.org/10.20535/2410-8286.60757

Harsch, C., & Rupp, A. A. (2011). Designing and scaling level-specific writing tasks in alignment with the CEFR: a test-centered approach. *Language Assessment Quarterly*, *8*(1), 1-33. https://doi.org/10.1080/15434303.2010.535575

Lenoir, Y. (1996). Médiation cognitive et médiation didactique. Le didactique au-delà des didactiques. *Débats autour de concepts fédérateurs*, 223-251.

Levy, M., & Stockwell, G. (1997). *CALL dimensions: options and issues in computer-assisted language learning*. Routledge.

Little, D. (2006). The common European framework of reference for languages: content, purpose, origin, reception and impact. *Language Teaching*, *39*(3), 167-190. https://doi.org/10.1017/s0261444806003557

Lowie, W. M., Haines, K. B., & Jansma, P. N. (2010). Embedding the CEFR in the academic domain: assessment of language tasks. *Procedia-Social and Behavioral Sciences*, *3*, 152-161. https://doi.org/10.1016/j.sbspro.2010.07.027

Mestre, E., & Pastor, M. L. C. (2013). A pragmatic perspective to leverage English for specific purposes. *Revista española de lingüística aplicada*, *1*, 229-244.

Stanford University. (2020, January). *An invitation to CALL foundations of computer-assisted language learning*. Stanford University. https://web.stanford.edu/~efs/callcourse2/CALL1.htm

Trim, J. (2012). Preface. In A. Green, *Language functions revisited: theoretical and empirical bases for language construct definition across the ability range* (vol. 2, p. xxi). Cambridge University Press.

Vygotsky, L. S. (1934). *The collected works of LS Vygotsky: problems of general psychology, including the volume thinking and speech* (vol. 1). Springer.

Weir, C. J. (2005). Limitations of the common European framework for developing comparable examinations and tests. *Language Testing*, *22*(3), 281-300. https://doi.org/10.1191/0265532205lt309oa

Yin, R. K. (2014). *Case study research: design and methods*. Sage publications.

2. Multimodal texts in support of linguistic and critical thinking development in English for specific purposes

Stavroulla Hadjiconstantinou[1]

Abstract

In light of widespread recognition of the need to explore new forms of literacy brought by the contemporary semiotic world, this study explores the potential Critical Thinking (CT) may offer in developing learners' critical literacy in an English for Specific Purposes (ESP) context enhanced with the use of technology. Drawing on research in critical pedagogy that highlights the importance of raising learners' critical awareness through language, I explore how critical practices of identifying and negotiating the expression of personal opinion in multimodal texts, in an English for the Media context particularly sensitive to issues of criticality, can enhance the development of multimodal literacy. This development is informed by Design-Based Research (DBR) (McKenney & Reeves, 2013), in which iteration and refinement of an intervention designed around these practices leads to the development of principles deriving from the evolution of the design.

Keywords: multimodal literacy, critical pedagogy, ESP.

---

1. Cyprus University of Technology, Limassol, Cyprus; s.hadjiconstantinou@cut.ac.cy; https://orcid.org/0000-0001-6226-8000

How to cite: Hadjiconstantinou, S. (2021). Multimodal texts in support of linguistic and critical thinking development in English for specific purposes. In S. Papadima-Sophocleous, E. Kakoulli Constantinou & C. N. Giannikas (Eds), *Tertiary education language learning: a collection of research* (pp. 29-45). Research-publishing.net. https://doi.org/10.14705/rpnet.2021.51.1253

Chapter 2

1. Introduction

The contemporary nature of the communicative semiotic landscape created by new technologies is highlighting the need to revisit our definition of literacy. To be considered literate in this day and age is to be able to effectively communicate multimodally, and this involves "human, cognitive/affective, cultural and bodily engagement with the world and on the forms and shapes of knowledge" (Kress, 2003, p.1). This multimodal shift relates to the understanding that language is no longer an independent code but is part of a set of semiotic resources that effectively 'synchronize' to communicate meaning. Part of the shift requires the literacy curriculum to evolve beyond the traditional domains, competencies, and skills. This work describes an instructional design informed by CT and pedagogy practices, aiming to develop students' ability to critically approach and reproduce information in support of multimodal literacy.

1.1. CT and critical literacy

Despite the widespread recognition of the significance of CT, literature from the field of education indicates that there is uncertainty in conceptualizing it, which may actually be linked to the challenge faced by educators with regards to the ways it should be developed (Ennis, 1985; Facione, 1990). In a discussion of the implications for teaching CT at university for example, Moore (2013) maintains that what is required are acquisition processes that are rooted within specific study contexts and that involve targeted acts of dialog and interaction included in teaching activities. Such efforts, as mentioned by Rezaei, Derakhshan, and Bagherkazemi (2011, p. 772) can be seen in the field of language education where using inferential questions to develop students' CT in the teaching of reading and writing is not uncommon. Some of these include Elder and Paul's (2004) effort to emphasize the importance of engaging oneself in constant questioning in the reading process. In a subsequent study Paul (2005) states that "a critical mind improves reading by reflectively thinking about what and how it reads"(p. 32) and finally Cook (1991) regards reading primarily as a thinking process and stresses the significance of engaging students in talking about the text they read. Research on the development of CT therefore indicates that it can only be cultivated through practices of thinking initiated and scaffolded by educators themselves through an understanding of the principles that govern CT in specific domains and an appropriation of teaching practices.

1.2. Critical needs in the media context

Needs analysis as one of the principles in the design and implementation of ESP courses, was conducted in the context of this study to identify and address the linguistic and CT needs of students in the media (Dudley-Evans & St John, 1998). Exploring CT practices, highlighted the term *critical media literacy*. This refers to the immense influence of Mass media and popular culture in transforming dominant ideologies, and emphasizes the development in learners of a critical eye toward how writers, illustrators, and in general creators of all kinds of texts create these texts and use them in promoting or suppressing particular views and ideas (Kellner & Share, 2007). More specifically, developing critical media literacy requires raising learners' awareness of the different messages transmitted through the media in various forms of representation and interaction. In developing such awareness, the concept of myside bias (Stanovich, West, & Toplak, 2013) as a construct of CT from Cognitive psychology was highlighted for its relevance to thinking and language practices particularly common in the media.

Beyond this, collaboration is considered particularly valuable in the context of ESP for the media, as developing critical media literacy skills involves learners in text negotiation and manipulation often requiring individual and collective analysis, deconstruction, and re-creation of materials from a variety of sources. Harasim, Hiltz, Teles, and Turoff (1995), define online collaborative learning as "a learning process where two or more people work together to create meaning, explore a topic, or improve skills" (p. 30). Recent advances in information and multimedia technologies contributing to the emergence of new literacy practices in online contexts (Hafner & Miller, 2011) further emphasize the need to develop pedagogical strategies for dealing with the abundance of multimodal data which learners in tertiary education are required to process, evaluate, share, and negotiate.

Chapter 2

1.3. Multimodality and multimodal literacy

Kress and van Leeuwen (2001) define multimodality as "the use of several semiotic modes in the design of a semiotic product or event" (p. 20). Dillon (2017) further states that it aims to "extend the social interpretation of language and its meanings to the [whole] range of representational and communicational modes for making meaning that are employed in a culture [including images, writing, body language, facial expressions]" (p. 55). Multimodal communication assumes an orchestration or co-deployment of all these meaning making, semiotic resources.

Over the last 85 years, the new literacy movement to refocus literacy as social practice brought profound changes in the use of these resources in education (Jewitt, 2006; Kress & van Leeuwen, 2001; Leander, 2002). The New London Group's (1996) argument on how literacy pedagogy must account for the diverse, dynamic, and multifaceted nature of communication texts and practices highlighted the need for example, to provide students with opportunities to create their own meanings and develop their personal voice in writing. Contrary to traditional instructional practices for writing (focusing on what is written), the need for student involvement and motivation (how and why something is written) is stressed. Beyond this the The New London Group's (1996) argument for "situated practice" (p. 85), is in line with critical engagement which, according to proponents of critical pedagogy, "promotes the development of student autonomy and control by [familiarizing] learners with explicit knowledge of language and genres" (Kiss & Mizusawa, 2018, p. 61).

Developing multimodal communication skills involves using language together with other multimodal resources to make meanings in different contexts. As stated by Ho and Lim (2020), this involves the development of fluency in "multimodal literacy [which] is about students learning to view multimodal texts critically and to communicate effectively through multimodal representations (Jewitt & Kress, 2003;Van Leeuwen, 2007)" (p. 254). In order to do this, students need to develop an understanding of how different semiotic resources work together to make meaning. This will then lead to developing students' ability to use text and other modalities to produce and represent meanings in different contexts. Multimodal learning supports collaborative authorship as it brings students together in pursuit of communicative objectives in support of contextualized acquisition of targeted language forms. A very important step toward that direction is the recognition of the social context created between those who make and those who engage with text. This consideration has been crucial in this work, which explored multimodality as a tool in critically analyzing this social context through the expression of opinion and bias in support of linguistic and thinking development.

Systemic Functional Linguistics (SFL) offered a sophisticated way of analyzing the relations between language and social contexts (Halliday, 1996).

1.4. Teaching multimodal literacy in the media context

1.4.1. The systemic functional approach

SFL, inspired by the work of Michael Halliday (1978) as one of the approaches to multimodality, provides learners and teachers with ways of exploring linguistic and other choices in relation to meaning through the analysis of multimodal texts. The pedagogical features of the systemic functional approach introduce learners to the social purpose of texts and develop their understanding of language through identification and discussion of specific features in these texts.

Apart from the socializing context, the repertoire representing an individual's access to the linguistic system is shaped by their identity, consciousness, and culture. Using these distinguishing characteristics to question and explore the connection between linguistic choices and the socializing context that guides them is a form of literacy – reflection literacy – that relates to the potential of language to create meaning (Hasan, 1996). O'Halloran, Palincsar, and Schleppegrell (2015) draw on Hasan's (1996) work focusing on the development in teachers and young children of critical awareness by introducing the notion of 'author attitude' in science texts. In a similar context, Achugar, Schleppegrell, and Oteiza (2007) explore three settings in which a reflective literacy approach is introduced to public school history teachers in the U.S. Raising teacher's awareness of the linguistic features characterizing historical texts provides them with tools to evaluate the texts learners read and write, and identify the challenges this type of text can pose for learners. The functional linguistics metalanguage they explore also enables teachers to value the discourses learners bring to the classroom and allows them to build on and expand learners' language repertoire. The need to enable this type of reflective literacy for students is recognized in this study, in which media learners draw on their background experience and knowledge to critically reflect and engage with the language used to discuss bias in an effort to raise awareness and further develop linguistic resources that characterize media texts.

1.4.2. Critical pedagogy

In the intervention described here, activities were designed to engage students in collaborative critical analysis of authentic multimodal texts which were based on explicit critical discussion of targeted linguistics and other resources used by authors to express opinion and bias. As a feature of critical pedagogy, critical and dialogic questioning (Benesch, 1999) is a concept inherent to CT. Research conducted in English for academic purposes contexts indicates that a dialogic approach to CT can cater for both the development of students' immediate academic needs and their right to negotiate the status quo by assuming new roles and responsibilities (Benesch, 1999; Morgan, 2009). Beyond this, transformative awareness emerges through activities in which students are encouraged to assume responsibility and construct critical insights in relation to situated requirements and their own needs and rights (Cadman, 2005). This study targets a co-development of both thinking and language through an exploration of the possibilities language and other modalities offer in the expression of biased thinking and, more specifically, myside bias in media texts. This endeavor is informed by critical and literacy practices facilitating a dialogic pedagogy of interrogation, reflection, and empowerment.

Various Information Technology (IT) tools were used to facilitate collaborative meaning making and artifact creation; among these, Moodle eLearning platform, Google Drive, and Facebook. Artifact creation is integral to the development of multimodal literacy as it enhances learning through making and provides ways for students to represent their learning (Lim, 2018). All of these considerations informed the evolution of a pedagogic design targeted at exploring multimodal literacy practices in support of students' linguistic development.

2. Method

As already mentioned, the research design developed in this study explored CT practices as the context in enhancing university media students' language through engagement with multimodal texts. The design targeted linguistic growth by engaging learners with practices of language identification, analysis, and manipulation, as well as the kind of thinking that can enhance the development of such practices and the language they require. The need to iterate and refine the emerging design has made DBR methodology appropriate for this study.

> "DBR is a methodology designed by and for educators that seeks to increase the impact, transfer, and translation of education research into improved practice (Barab & Squire, 2004). In addition, it stresses the need for theory building and the development of design principles that guide, inform, and improve both practice and research in educational contexts" (Anderson & Shattuck, 2012, p.16).

The design reflected the outcome of the needs analysis and was refined through three cycles of enactment, data collection, analysis, and revision.

2.1. Research context and participants

The study was conducted with students in the Faculty of Communication and Media Studies. Students in this department attend three compulsory ESP language courses (English for the Media Studies I, II, III) as part of their four

Chapter 2

year undergraduate degree. Participants were 40 Greek-Cypriot and three Erasmus students aged between 19-21 years and who were assessed at an upper-intermediate level of English – Common European Framework of Reference (CEFR) B2-C1. All Greek-Cypriot participants were native speakers of Greek and studied English as a second language for at least six years during their primary and secondary education. They also attended private English language institutes for an average of five years. Erasmus students had a similar English language competence level.

2.2. The design

The pedagogic design, comprising of tasks, materials, and tools was iterated in three cycles of implementation, assessment and redesign (adapted from Reeves, 2006, p. 59). In the cycles, the design becomes reified through dialogic activities resulting in the production of artifacts. In the activities, specific linguistic resources (nominalization, use of voice, reported speech, and modality) are foregrounded and related to thinking and the expression of bias. Each cycle includes a research and a redesign phase. In the research phase, artifacts, participants' views on these, as well as instructor's reflections and observations, are analyzed and re-examined in light of the theory framing the study so as to contribute to the development of students' language and thinking through the generation of new research objectives. In the redesign phase, the revised research objectives inform the new cycle by redefining the tasks, materials, tools, and methodology to be employed. In the center of each cycle, language and thinking practices move the design by slightly shifting the orientation of each cycle (research objectives).

2.3. Data collection and analysis methods

The first phase of data collection explored present (academic) and target situation (professional) needs of students in the specific area of studies. These were identified by the students themselves and academic members of their faculty through questionnaires administered to all participants as well as a semi-structured focus group with the academic staff to discuss the findings from the questionnaires and explore issues arising in more detail. Following initial needs analysis of the data, I evaluated and redesigned the syllabus of the existing program. The second phase of data collection was concerned with the implementation and evaluation of the design. As the development of the initial design evolved through the implementation cycles, I collected data using different instruments. These included a researcher's journal, field notes in the form of instructional logs, questionnaires, and focus groups with the participants, student reflections, and student artifacts (text data).

Transcribed data from focus groups with students; the researcher's journal, as well as field notes and students' reflections, were read thoroughly, and emerging themes were recorded as nodes and linked to text from the dataset with the use of N-vivo qualitative data analysis software. More precisely, every time a new set of data was analyzed emerging themes were examined and compared to existing ones so as to add new codes and merge recurrent ones with the coding system already created in N-vivo. Throughout this process, insights and ideas emerging from the data were reported as memos within N-vivo to ensure that the theoretical ideas that have emerged in the first round of coding can be systematically evidenced in the data.

For each group of data analyzed, emerging codes were explored in light of the theory framing the study. By moving back and forth between data, further theoretical concepts and patterns emerged, and so I refined preliminary codes by removing overlapping ones. A dynamic audit trail was created through N-vivo's built-in tools for recording and connecting data from various sources so as to meet the criterion of transparency and to enhance confidence in findings (Bringer, Johnston, & Brackenridge, 2004).

Targeted linguistic and other resources, and their role in affecting ways of thinking and talking about bias, were analyzed with the use of SFL as a system of choices (Halliday, 1978) in student final online articles. Based on this theory, I used the system of transitivity to analyze instances of language in terms of participants and processes and to examine their role in creating meaning. I also used the system of modality realized in the mood part of a clause (subject and finite) and explored by the interpersonal meta function (Bloor & Bloor, 2013; Matthiessen & Halliday, 2014). This allowed me to explore students' understanding of the functions of the metalanguage used as an indication of their linguistic development.

Additionally, I analyzed tasks with regards to students' critical understanding and use of multimodal components, in particular images, in their work to encode personal opinion. I used Kress and van Leeuwen's (1996) ways of constructing and maintaining interaction between the producer and the viewer of an image as described in their work on representation, interaction, and modality. According to this, a number of features in an image can be used to analyse the relational and interactional or interpersonal processes that take place between represented participants (the people, places, things depicted in images) and interactive participants (the people who communicate through the images, the producer, and the viewer). To evaluate students' understanding of these features as explained and discussed in class, I used the following criteria to assess the images students used to complement their texts.

- Image act: the gaze and/or gestures of represented participants

This relates to represented participants' direct or indirect look or gesture at the viewer. Such features in an image firstly create a visual form of direct and formal address and secondly, they indicate a requirement for the viewer to enter into some kind of imaginary relation with him or her. Exactly what kind of relation is then signified by other means, such as the facial expression or the gesture used.

- Social distance: size of frame and angle

The choice between close up, medium, and long shot (size of frame) allows for different degrees of viewer involvement with the represented participants. They can allow us as viewers to come close or distance ourselves from represented participants. At close distance the object is shown as if the viewer is engaged with it, whereas at long distance there is a barrier between the viewer and the object.

- Modality

Visuals can represent people, places, and things as though they are real, as though they actually exist in a specific way or not. The more that is taken away (from an image), abstracted from the colors of the representation, the more color is reduced and the lower the modality.

3. Results and discussion

Analysis of data from the researcher's journal, field notes, students' reflections, and focus groups indicated participants' appreciation of the affordances of the design in developing learners' ability to use text and other multimodal components based on their functional use to express opinion. Specifically, based on the final round of qualitative coding analysis in N-vivo, the following three categories detailed by a number of recurrent (sub-)themes indicate trends in the data and sometimes overlap between the categories emerged.

Critical mindset in support of language and thinking development was the first recurrent category, and it related to the CT and literacy practices incorporated into the design of activities, which were informed by the construct of myside bias (Toplak & Stanovich, 2003). This, as already mentioned, has been a fundamental concept framing this study both theoretically and empirically. Based on findings indicating that the avoidance of myside bias is a result of practice and that it is positively correlated to a facilitating environment (Stanovich & West, 2008), the designed activities targeted language development through linguistic practices of identifying, discussing, and controlling such modes of thinking. In the activities, iteration of a standardized critical questioning procedure, enhanced by scaffolds targeting specific content and linguistic elements in texts, enabled the gradual development of a critical mindset in learners. Through their repeated employment, these resources (CT and linguistic), initially employed as a point of reference in the activities, gradually developed beyond a set of instructions into practices of thinking.

Chapter 2

The potential of *Language as a tool in the development of both thinking and linguistic competence* emerged as the second main recurrent category in the data. This was associated to an understanding of the functional role of language and other resources in expressing attitude as part of a wider development in language as perceived by the learners.

Finally, the use of *Dialog in support of language and thinking development* was supported by recurrent themes in the data deriving from theories on critical pedagogy, as well as shifts in both students' and the teacher's thinking with regards to refined classroom practices, engagement, and competence. As mentioned earlier, critical pedagogy was used in the study to facilitate learners' engagement with text in the context created by CT practices and more specifically the avoidance of myside bias. Through this engagement, discussions on texts were used to raise learner's critical awareness of the relationship between linguistic and other resources and meaning (Durant & Lambrou, 2009).

Other important benefits to linguistic improvement from practices of dialogic engagement, recorded as recurrent themes in the data, related to new measurements of achievement, instant constructive feedback, and collaboration within the dialogic community. More specifically, a number of learners highlighted that by taking part in the discussions they were able to observe and adapt good practices exhibited by more competent students. They were also supported through feedback from the instructor and their peers, and this enhanced both their level of engagement and performance.

Multimodality, supported by the use of technology which was key in the design of activities, was also acknowledged by participants for its contribution in complementing text to improve writing.

> "I think the use of image was also really useful…there is so much information in an image or video and this lesson showed us how images can be used in combination with writing to make a piece more powerful…".

Authenticity enhanced by the use of multimodal material was also acknowledged by some learners.

> "In our discussion of different issues, it was very interesting that we watched real life videos of people talking about these issues, speaking in a certain way, emphasizing certain words using specific language to support their views...which we later identified with our critical analysis".

In the quote above, the student identifies and comments on his engagement with 'real life' material through which he is enabled to observe peoples' speech and use of specific words to support ideas. It is interesting to note the student's recognition of how this experience supported their work in critical analysis.

Another finding on multimodality related to students' appreciation of the use of multimodal texts as an additional way of understanding and representing meaning.

> "I am a visual learner so I think I have benefitted from learning to critically analyze and use images... I can communicate meaning better now!"

What is interesting in the reflection above is the student's acknowledgment of how multimodal literacy builds on characteristics of their learning style by providing a preferred mode of representation, allowing for more powerful learning.

4. Conclusion

As indicated in the characteristics of DBR, research should target the evolution of principles. Systematic and ongoing analysis of data, collected through iteration of the designed intervention in this study, led to the generation of design principles relating to theory, pedagogy, and methodology which may be operationalized in other contexts.

Specifically, analysis of the data highlighted that identifying learners' CT and literacy skills can be useful in creating the social context around which language engagement can be made meaningful in support of language development. Furthermore, drawing on specific concepts from SFL to foreground the relationship between language and thinking, in this study in expressing personal opinion, can support teachers and learners in understanding how language works, and can support both linguistic teaching and learning. Moreover, data analysis has shown that understanding the functional role of language and other modalities in construing meaning (e.g. avoiding bias) is an important parameter in sustaining rationality and critical thought, and that iteration of critical questioning processes can develop habits of mind which seem to support both learners' thinking and language. Specifically, developing students' understanding of how different semiotic resources work together to express opinion/bias can help in advancing their ability to use text and other modalities in producing and representing meaning in different contexts.

Finally, analysis of data indicated that critical engagement with language through multimodal texts can enhance collaboration among learners in support of meaningful interaction and linguistic growth.

References

Achugar, M., Schleppegrell, M., & Oteiza, T. (2007). Engaging teachers in language analysis: a functional linguistics approach to reflective literacy. *English Teaching, 6*(2), 8-24.

Anderson, T., & Shattuck, J. (2012). Design-based research: a decade of progress in education research? *Educational Researcher, 41*(1), 16-25. https://doi.org/10.3102/0013189X11428813

Barab, S., & Squire, K. (2004). Design-based research: putting a stake in the ground. *The Journal of the Learning Sciences, 13*(1), 1-14. https://doi.org/10.1207/s15327809jls1301_1

Benesch, S. (1999). Thinking critically, thinking dialogically. *Tesol Quarterly, 33*(3), 573-580. https://doi.org/10.2307/3587682

Bloor, T., & Bloor, M. (2013). *The functional analysis of English: a Hallidayan approach.* Routledge.

Bringer, J. D., Johnston, L. H., & Brackenridge, C. H. (2004). Maximizing transparency in a doctoral thesis1: the complexities of writing about the use of QSR* NVIVO within a grounded theory study. *Qualitative Research, 4*(2), 247-265. https://doi.org/10.1177/1468794104044434

Cadman, K. (2005). Towards a "pedagogy of connection" in critical research education: a REAL story. *Journal of English for Academic Purposes, 4*(4), 353-367. https://doi.org/10.1016/j.jeap.2005.07.001

Cook, J. E. (1991). Critical reading? *How? Why? Teaching Prek-, 21*(6), 23-24.

Dillon. A. (2017). *Scripture and its reception: a semiotic analysis of selected graphic designs illustrating biblical lections in iconic liturgical books.* Doctoral thesis. Dublin City University. http://doras.dcu.ie/22149/1/AMANDADILLONthesissml.pdf

Dudley-Evans, T., & St John, M. J. (1998). *Developments in English for specific purposes: a multi-disciplinary approach.* Cambridge university press.

Durant, A., & Lambrou, M. (2009). *Language and media: a resource book for students.* Routledge.

Elder, L., & Paul, R. (2004). Critical thinking and the art of close reading (part 2). *Journal of Developmental Education, 27*(3), 36-37.

Ennis, R. H. (1985). A logical basis for measuring critical thinking skills. *Educational Leadership, 43*(2), 44-48.

Facione, P. A. (1990). *Critical thinking: a statement of expert consensus for purposes of educational assessment and instruction.* Research Findings and Recommendations.

Hafner, C. A., & Miller, L. (2011). Fostering learner autonomy in English for science: a collaborative digital video project in a technological learning environment. *Language Learning & Technology, 15*(3), 68-86.

Halliday, M. A. K. (1978). *Language as social semiotic.* The Open University.

Halliday, M. A. K. (1996). Literacy and linguistics: a functional perspective. In R. Hasan & G. Williams (Eds), *Literacy in society* (pp. 339-376). Longman.

Harasim, L. M., Hiltz, S. R., Teles, L., & Turoff, M. (1995). *Learning networks: a field guide to teaching and learning online.* MIT Press.

Hasan, R. (1996). Literacy, everyday talk and society. *Language and education: learning and teaching in society - The Collected Works of Ruqaiya Hasan* (vol 3, pp. 169-206). Equinox eBooks Publishing.

Ho, C., & Lim, F. V. (2020). Assessing conceptual understanding in primary science through students' multimodal representations in science notebooks. In T. W. Teo, A.-L. Tan, & Y. S. Ong (Eds), *Science education in the 21st century* (pp. 153-167). Springer.

Jewitt, C. (2006). *Technology, literacy and learning: a multimodal approach*. Psychology Press.

Jewitt, C., & Kress, G. (2003). *A multimodal approach to research in education*. Trentham Books in association with the Open University.

Kellner, D., & Share, J. (2007). Critical media literacy, democracy, and the reconstruction of education. In D. Macedo & S. R. Steinberg (Eds), *Media literacy: a reader* (pp. 3-23). Peter Lang.

Kiss, T., & Mizusawa, K. (2018). Revisiting the pedagogy of multiliteracies: writing instruction in a multicultural context. *Changing English, 25*(1), 59-68. https://doi.org/10.1080/1358684x.2017.1403283

Kress, G. (2003). *Literacy in the new media age*. Routledge.

Kress, G., & van Leeuwen, T. (1996). *Reading images: the grammar of visual design*. Psychology Press.

Kress, G., & van Leeuwen, T. (2001). *Multimodal discourse: the modes and media of contemporary communication*. Arnold.

Leander, K. M. (2002). Locating Latanya: the situated production of identity artifacts in classroom interaction. *Research in the Teaching of English, 37*, 198-250.

Lim, F. V. (2018). Developing a systemic functional approach to teach multimodal literacy. *Functional Linguistics, 5*(13), 1-17. https://doi.org/10.1186/s40554-018-0066-8

Matthiessen, C., & Halliday, M. A. (2014). *Halliday's introduction to functional grammar*. Routledge.

McKenney, S., & Reeves, T. C. (2013). *Conducting educational design research*. Routledge.

Moore, T. (2013). Critical thinking: seven definitions in search of a concept. *Studies in Higher Education, 38*(4), 506-522. https://doi.org/10.1080/03075079.2011.586995

Morgan, B. (2009). Revitalising the essay in an English for academic purposes course: critical engagement, multiliteracies and the internet. *International Journal of Bilingual Education and Bilingualism, 12*(3), 309-324. https://doi.org/10.1080/13670050802153350

O'Hallaron, C. L., Palincsar, A. S., & Schleppegrell, M. J. (2015). Reading science: using systemic functional linguistics to support critical language awareness. *Linguistics and Education, 32*, 55-67. https://doi.org/10.1016/j.linged.2015.02.002

Paul, R. (2005). The state of critical thinking today. *New Directions for Community Colleges, 2005*(130), 27-38. https://doi.org/10.1002/cc.193

Reeves, T. C. (2006). Design research from a technology perspective. *Educational Design Research, 1*(3), 52-66.

Rezaei, S., Derakhshan, A., & Bagherkazemi, M. (2011). Critical thinking in language education. *Journal of Language Teaching and Research, 2*(4), 769-777. https://doi.org/10.4304/jltr.2.4.769-777

Stanovich, K. E, & West, R. F. (2008). On the relative independence of thinking biases and cognitive ability. *Journal of Personality and Social Psychology, 94*(4), 672-695. https://doi.org/10.1037/0022-3514.94.4.672

Stanovich, K. E., West, R. F., & Toplak, M. E. (2013). Myside bias, rational thinking, and intelligence. *Current Directions in Psychological Science, 22*(4), 259-264. https://doi.org/10.1177/0963721413480174

The New London Group. (1996). A pedagogy of multiliteracies: designing social futures. *Harvard Educational Review, 66*(1), 60-93. https://doi.org/10.17763/haer.66.1.17370n67v22j160u

Toplak, M. E., & Stanovich, K. E. (2003). Associations between myside bias on an informal reasoning task and amount of post-secondary education. *Applied Cognitive Psychology, 17*(2), 851-860. https://doi.org/10.1002/acp.915

Van Leeuwen, T. (2007). Legitimation in discourse and communication. *Discourse & Communication, 1*(1), 91-112. https://doi.org/10.1177/1750481307071986

Students' attitudes towards digital artefact creation through collaborative writing: the case of a Spanish for specific purposes class

María Victoria Soulé[1]

Abstract

Studies on collaborative writing practices are not new (Reynolds, Wooley, & Wooley, 1911), neither is the interest in collaborative writing supported by computers (Sharples, 1993). With the advent of Web 2.0, there has been an immense increase in research examining web-based collaborative writing, particularly in L2 contexts (Cho, 2017; Kessler, 2013; Sevilla-Pavón, 2015; Yim & Warschauer, 2017). The present study follows this research path by analysing perceptions of technology-assisted collaborative writing as well as collaborative writing processes in a Spanish for specific purposes class. Eight students from the Cyprus University of Technology (CUT), Department of Communication and Internet Studies, participated in the study. The data were elicited over five collection times, which included two digital artefact creations (an out-of-class and an in-class collaborative writing task), a pre-Questionnaire (preQ) and post-Questionnaire (postQ), and a focus group interview. The analysis of the data revealed that the students' perceptions are mediated by task type, which in turn also affects collaborative writing patterns being the out-of-class activity the one that presents a wider variety of writing styles as well as a more balanced participation among students.

Keywords: digital artefact creation, collaborative writing, Google Docs, L2 Spanish.

---

1. Cyprus University of Technology, Limassol, Cyprus; mariavictoria.soule@cut.ac.cy; https://orcid.org/0000-0001-7798-2426

How to cite: Soulé, M. V. (2021). Students' attitudes towards digital artefact creation through collaborative writing: the case of a Spanish for specific purposes class. In S. Papadima-Sophocleous, E. Kakoulli Constantinou & C. N. Giannikas (Eds), *Tertiary education language learning: a collection of research* (pp. 47-63). Research-publishing.net. https://doi.org/10.14705/rpnet.2021.51.1354

Chapter 3

1. Introduction

In recent years we have observed that the advance of collaborative culture has transformed the way in which we communicate. Kessler (2013) points out that despite the fact that the nature of our communication practices has changed outside education "it seems there is little reflection on the potential that these changes have to offer to language teaching and learning" (p. 313). However, he also recognises that there has been a significant amount of interest in the collaborative construction of knowledge, particularly in writing, within contemporary technology contexts. This interest has been reflected in many studies that explore the nature of collaborative writing from different perspectives. For instance, early research discussed designs for synchronous and asynchronous collaborative writing through computer mediated communication and group editor applications from a conceptual model of cooperative work (Miles et al., 1993).

More recently, Cho (2017) investigated synchronous web-based collaborative writing and the factors that mediated interaction among language learners. The author claimed that (1) modes of communication (text-chat and synchronous voice-chat), (2) task representations, "set of rules that regulated and guided the subject's actions and interactions" (Cho, 2017, p. 47), (3) matches/mismatches between participants' self-perceived, and (4) other perceived roles and perceptions of peer feedback were the mediating factors on the quality of the collaboration. Another study that explored synchronous and asynchronous collaborative and collective writing was conducted by Sevilla-Pavón (2015). The author examined collective authorship and collaborative writing within a digital storytelling project carried out in a technical English class of aerospace engineering. She found that collaboration and collective writing allowed her students to assume different roles at different times: *writer, editor, reviewer, team leader,* and *facilitator.*

Wang et al. (2015a), using a document visualisation tool called DocuViz (Wang et al., 2015b), analysed how students from a project management class wrote collaboratively using Google Docs. The authors found three patterns of collaboration: *outline, example,* and *best-of-each.* More recently, Olson, Wang, Zhang, and Olson (2017), also using DocuViz, analysed the use of Google

Docs among engineering undergraduate majors. They found six patterns of collaborations: *from scratch, outline, assignment, example, assign people*, and *informal discussion*. Yim et al. (2017) examined the impact of synchronous collaborative writing in student's writing style, quality, and quantity. The analysis of their data revealed four styles of writing: *main writer, divide and conquer, cooperative revision,* and *synchronous hands-on*. The researchers highlighted that the "Divide and Conquer style tended to produce better quality text, particularly in content and evidence, whereas Main Writer style had the lowest scores in those areas" (Yim et al., 2017, p. 476). As for quantity and quality, they claimed that "[b]alanced participation and active editing behaviours predicted better writing quality (e.g. content, evidence, lexical frequency) and quantity" (Yim et al., 2017, p. 476).

As Yim and Warschauer (2017) synthesised in their study of current methodological approaches to researching collaborative writing, research has mainly focused on collaborative writing outcomes, perceptions of collaborative writing, and collaborative writing processes. The present study focuses on the last two research strands. In particular, we explore students' attitudes towards digital artefact creation through collaborative writing in a Spanish for specific purposes class. The study steps on the learning theory of constructionism (Papert, 1980, 1993; Papert & Harel, 1991) defined as:

> "[i]ncluding, but going beyond, what Piaget would call 'constructivism'. The word with the *v* expresses the theory that knowledge is built by the learner, not supplied by the teacher. The word with the *n* expresses the further idea that this happens especially felicitously when the learner is engaged in the construction of something external or at least shareable [...] a sand castle, a machine, a computer program, a book" (Papert & Harel, 1991, p. 1).

Within the constructionism theory, Resnick (1996) introduces the concept of *distributed constructionism* based on the use of computer networks to support students working together on design and construction activities. According to Resnick (1996), distributed constructionism is characterised by three

Chapter 3

categories: discussing constructions, sharing constructions, and collaborating on constructions. The first one is illustrated through the use of a forum for discussing construction activities. The second one is exemplified through texts, images, or videos that can be copied and/or reused by others. And the third category involves the use of computer networks to support students "not only to share ideas with one another, but to collaborate directly, in real time, on the design and construction projects" (Resnick, 1996, p. 282).

The theory of constructionism has been applied to some extent to language learning studies (Rüschoff, 2004; Rüschoff & Ritter, 2001), with some of them investigating collaborative writing practices (Parmaxi & Zaphiris, 2015; Parmaxi, Zaphiris, & Ioannou, 2016). However, there is no study up to date that has been conducted within this theory to investigate students' perceptions of collaborative writing and collaborative writing processes. The present study aims to fill this gap. More specifically, the study addresses the following research questions.

- What are students' initial beliefs and attitudes regarding collaborative writing with the use of technology in a Spanish for specific purposes class?

- Do students' attitudes towards collaborative writing evolve and change after collaborative writing experiences with the use of technology?

- To what extent are students' beliefs and attitudes reflected on their actual collaborative writing practices?

2. Method

2.1. Research design

To address these research questions, a mixed-method case study approach was employed. This methodology combines a quantitative research component with qualitative case study, where the former provides an objective assessment of learners' attitudes towards collaborative writing and actual collaborative writing practices, and the latter aims to understand and interpret the behaviours of individual learners (Duff, 2008).

2.2. Context and participants

The research was carried out at the Language Centre of the CUT, within the Spanish 2 (LCE 631) course. This is an elective course that concentrates on the learning of Spanish for academic purposes. The general objective of the course is to enable students to communicate in Spanish at the level A1+/A2 of the Common European Framework of Reference (CEFR) on issues related to the students' field of studies. The course is based on the use of new technologies for teaching and learning purposes.

Eight students from the CUT Department of Communication and Internet Studies, participated in the study. The mean age of all the participants at the start of data collection was 22.62 (range 22-23) with four males and four females. Participation in this study was voluntary. The participants of the study were anonymised with the use of pseudonyms (Nespor, 2000).

2.3. Instruments

The instrumentation consisted of students' digital artefacts, preQ and postQ, and a focus group interview. Students' digital artefacts consisted of two collaborative writing tasks. The first one focused on a descriptive writing activity in the context of publishing a project. More specifically, students were divided in groups in order to write asynchronously collaborative texts that described Cypriot cities using Google Docs. It was an out-of-class activity. At a later stage, students converted their documents into an interactive publication using the digital magazine Calameo[2]. The second collaborative task consisted of writing a text synchronously. This text focused on historical buildings in the Cypriot city of Limassol. This was an in-class activity. The text was later used to produce a video of those buildings.

---

2. https://en.calameo.com/

Chapter 3

The preQ and postQ were used to measure change in students' attitudes towards collaborative writing after two collaborative writing experiences in a Spanish for specific purposes class. The questionnaires, adapted from Gökçe (2001), included open-ended questions and a rating scale. In the 16 items from the rating scale, students were asked to rate their perceptions towards collaborative writing based on a five-point Likert scale (1=completely disagree, 2=disagree, 3=neutral, 4=agree, 5=completely agree). The items from the scale were presented beneath the heading *What do you think about digital artefact creation through collaborative writing?*.

The focus group interview was selected as an instrument to explore students' beliefs about collaborative writing with Web 2.0 technologies. The interview was set up with a small group of eight participants and lasted about 25 minutes. Group interaction was based on a list of questions pertaining to the results of the preQ and postQ as well as the data obtained from the digital artefacts.

2.4. Data collection

The current study was longitudinal. The data collection process lasted two months and involved five data collection points. The five data collection times are shown in the diagram in Figure 1.

Figure 1. Data collections times

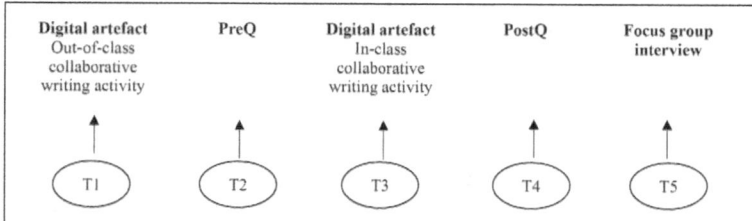

2.5. Data analysis

Students' digital artefacts were analysed with DocuViz, a tool that displays the entire revision history of Google Docs and investigates the patterns of collaborative creation of documents (Wang et al., 2015b). Quantitative data, mainly frequencies and percentages, were analysed for three categories: *contribution, edit of self*, and *edit of other*.

The quantitative data from the questionnaire were analysed with SPSS 26. Mean (M) and Standard Deviation (SD) were used to show differences from the preQ to the postQ. In addition, the paired-samples *t*-test was performed to identify if any variation in the students' responses were significantly different (Larson-Hall, 2010). Negatively worded items were reversed before analysis (Dörney, 2010). The open-ended questions were coded according to the analysis of data reduction, which involves first and second level coding, resulting in groups of categories followed by a quantitative analysis.

The qualitative data from the focus group interview were digitally recorded, translated from Greek into English, and transcribed, followed by the analysis of themes (or key issues) that emerged from students' responses "not for generalising beyond the case, but for understanding the complexity of the case" (Creswell, 2007, p. 75).

3. Results and discussion

3.1. Results from students' digital artefacts

The analysis of the students' digital artefacts illustrates the students' attitudes towards collaborative writing. The patterns of collaborative creation obtained from the Google Docs with DocuViz for the out-of-class collaborative writing activity are displayed in Table 1.

Table 1. Results from the out-of-class collaborative writing activity

Group	Participant	Contribution		Edit of self		Edit of other	
		N	%	N	%	N	%
G1	Anna	1,625	87.7	3,575	81.57	0	0
	Stavria	228	12.3	808	18.43	432	100

G2	Demetra	1,048	53.72	4,066	70.24	44	83.02
	Sophia	903	46.28	1,723	29.76	9	16.98
G3	Aristos	2001	47.27	2,683	50.29	22	5.1
	Spyros	2,232	52.73	2,652	49.71	409	94.9
G4	Pablo	2,086	79.92	5,665	83.43	61	10.95
	Giason	524	20.08	1,125	16.57	496	89.05

Table 1 shows two main tendencies in the out-of-class collaborative writing activity: (1) unbalanced participation, as in G1 and G4, and (2) balanced participation, as in G2 and G3. The first category presents the characteristics of the *main writer* style (Yim et al., 2017) where a main writer, Anna (G1) and Pablo (G4), dominates, while the other writers, Stavria (G1) and Giason (G4), barely contribute (see Figure 2a). In the balanced participation category, two paths can be observed: the first one is depicted by the *cooperative revision* style (Yim et al., 2017) where each writer writes their own part and freely edits each other's text, as in G2 (see Figure 2b), and the second path is described by the *synchronous hands-on* style where "members create sentences together by simultaneously building up on each other's text" (Yim et al., 2017, p. 473), as in G3. Interestingly, this group, even though the activity had been assigned to be completed out-of-class, decided to work synchronously.

Figure 2. (2a) Collaborative writing patterns of G1 during the out-of-class activity: *main writer* style[3]; (2b) collaborative writing patterns of G2 during the out-of-class activity: *cooperative revision* style[4]

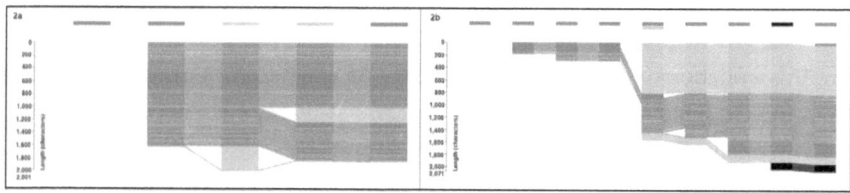

3. According to the developers of DocuViz: "each column represents the document at that moment with authorship of the segments of text noted in colour. The height of the bar represents the amount of text; successive columns represent time moving left to right. The sections between columns help the eye track the placement of text over time plus the additions and deletions. Additions are right facing openings; deletions are right facing contractions. Moves are blocks of identical text that have been repositioned. They are shown with a crossing bar between slices. The little bar at the top of the columns shows by colour who was present in that slice of time" (Wang et al., 2015a, p. 1869).

4. See supplementary materials for bigger screenshots

Regarding collaborative writing practices from the second task, which was completed by the students in the classroom, variations in students' collaborative writing patterns were observed. Results from this task are displayed in Table 2.

Table 2. Results from the in-class collaborative writing activity

Group	Participant	Contribution		Edit of self		Edit of other	
		N	%	N	%	N	%
G1	Anna	280	67.96	573	62.55	98	42.24
	Pablo	97	23.54	297	32.42	87	37.50
	Stavria	35	8.5	46	5.02	47	20.26
G2	Sophia	375	91.02	670	95.99	43	51.19
	Demetra	37	8.98	28	4.01	41	48.81
G3	Spyros	1,010	92.92	1,032	89.51	0	0
	Aristos	77	7.08	121	10.49	10	100

Results from Table 2 show a change in the collaborative writing patterns for G2 and G3, which moved from the balanced participation category (during the out-of-class activity) to the unbalanced participation category (during the in-class activity). G1 remains in the same category, with Anna again as the *main writer*, despite the incorporation of Pablo, who during the out-of-class activity was also the *main writer* of his group (G4). This tendency is negatively interpreted by some participants, as it will be shown in the responses from the open-ended questions where 57.1% of the students complained about unbalanced workload.

Another characteristic of the in-class collaborative writing activity is that only G2 presents an equal amount of peer editing, introducing some of the features of the *cooperative revision* style. Interestingly, in G3 the two members seem to have assumed two distinct main roles (Sevilla-Pavón, 2015): *writer*, as in the case of Spyros with 92.92% of the contribution to the task and the *editor-reviewer*, as in the case of Aristos with 100% of the editing of other.

Figure 3a and Figure 3b illustrate the tendencies of the in-class collaborative writing activity.

Figure 3. (3a) Collaborative writing patterns of G1 during the in-class activity: *main writer* and *synchronous hands-on* styles combined; (3b) collaborative writing patterns of G2 during the in-class activity: *main writer* and *synchronous hands-on* styles combined[5]

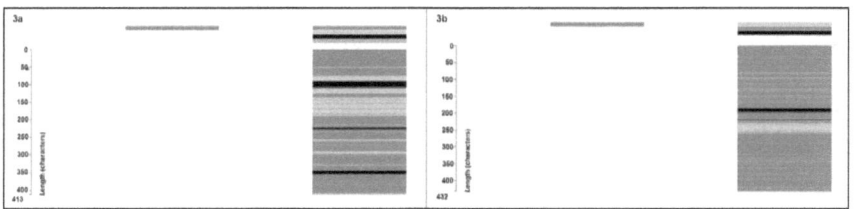

3.2. Results from the questionnaires

Results from the preQ and postQ show statistically significant differences in only one item out of the 16 that constitute the rating scale, asking about students' perceptions on digital artefact creation through collaborative writing. This item (Q15: "Disagreements in my group demotivated me") was related to the lack of motivation for collaborative writing given to disagreements among the members of a group.

For the paired-samples *t*-test (preQ $M=3.75$, $SD=1.28$; postQ $M=4.37$, $SD=1.06$) the 95% CI for the difference in means is -1.247, -.002 ($t=-2.376$, $p=.049$, $df=7$). The scores for this item represent a reverse-coded Likert scale score, in which the converted score, slightly below 4 for the preQ and above 4 for the postQ, represents the Likert scale point 2.0 or Disagree. This indicates that participants' motivation did not change despite groups' disagreement.

Table 3 displays the results for the remaining items where significant differences were not found.

---

5. See supplementary materials for bigger screenshots

Table 3. PreQ and postQ' results on students' perceptions towards digital artefact creation through collaborative writing

Questions	PreQ		PostQ		Paired-Samples t-test results			
	M	SD	M	SD	95% CI		t-value	p-value
Q1: I'd rather write with a group than alone.	3.38	1.06	2.75	0.89	-.141	1.391	1.930	.095
Q2: I got the chance to express my views in the group.	3.63	0.92	3.88	0.99	-1.411	.911	-.509	.626
Q3: Writing together we spent more time planning papers than I do when I write alone.	3.25	1.28	2.75	0.89	-.841	1.841	.882	.407
Q4: Writing together we spent more time checking spelling, punctuation, and grammar than I do when I write alone.	3.38	1.06	3.5	1.2	-1.498	1.248	-.215	.836
Q5: Every member of the group worked equally in writing the paper.	3.25	1.58	3.5	1.41	-1.966	1.466	-.344	.741
Q6: I learned new ways to brainstorm from my group.	3.63	1.06	3.13	0.99	-.499	1.499	1.183	.275
Q7: I learned new ways to plan writing from my group.	3.25	1.04	3	1.2	-1.072	1.572	.447	.668
Q8: I learned new ways to organise a paper from my group.	3.5	0.93	3	1.07	-.499	1.499	1.183	.275
Q9: I would like to write in a group again.	3.38	1.06	3	0.93	-.058	.808	2.049	.080
Q10: It is interesting to share ideas and write about them.	3.75	1.28	3.88	1.25	-1.423	1.173	-.228	.826
Q11: I felt more confident in group.	3.25	1.28	2.63	1.19	-.853	2.103	1.000	.351
Q12: Writing with my group had positive effects on my motivation.	3.25	1.16	3.38	1.19	-.954	.704	-.357	.732
Q13: Writing in a group did not help to improve my writing skills.	3.12	1.13	3.25	1.49	-1.344	1.094	-.243	.815

| Q14: Our writing was more creative in group writing. | 4 | 0.76 | 3.5 | 1.2 | -.499 | 1.499 | 1.183 | .275 |
| Q16: Group members learned something from me. | 2.88 | 1.25 | 2.75 | 1.16 | -1.094 | 1.344 | .243 | .815 |

The results presented in Table 3 can be divided into two groups: (1) increased positive attitudes towards digital artefact creation through collaborative writing in postQ, and (2) decreased positive attitudes towards digital artefact creation through collaborative writing in postQ. The first group includes items 2, 4, 5, 10, and 13 which were related to collective writing roles, work distribution, script copyediting, sharing ideas, and motivation. The opposite direction is represented by items 1, 3, 6, 7, 8, 9, 11, 14, and 15. These items are related to willingness to work in a group again, planning stages, boosting confidence, and creative writing.

Two open-ended questions from the questionnaires provide a preliminary explanation for these results. The first one, which asked about the positive aspects of group writing, reveals that 'exchange of opinions and ideas' was considered as one of the most valuable aspects of collaborative writing (preQ: 60%, postQ: 44.4%), followed by 'applicability in the future workplace' (preQ: 20%, postQ: 11.1%), 'equal work distribution' (preQ: 10%, postQ: 11.1%), 'improvement of writing skills' (preQ: 10%, postQ: 22.2%), and 'motivation' (postQ: 11.1%). The second open-ended question, related to negative aspects of group writing, shows an important percentage of students complaining about 'unbalanced workload' (preQ: 57.1%, postQ: 44.4%), followed by 'disagreement among group members' (preQ: 14.3%, postQ: 33.3%), 'incompatible working schedules' (preQ: 14.3%, 11.1%), 'fear of expressing one's thoughts' (preQ: 14.3%), and 'different level of knowledge among team members' (postQ: 11.1%).

3.3. Results from the focus group interview

The focus group interview took place in order to clarify students' responses from the questionnaires and collaborative writing patterns observed in the Google

Docs. The topics discussed included writing roles, script copyediting, sharing ideas, and motivation that in the postQ obtained higher positive perceptions from the students, as well as planning stages, willingness to work in a group again, boosting confidence, and creative writing that received higher negative perceptions in the postQ.

During the interview the writing roles topic was highlighted, as Demetra says "[w]e usually organise this [task], we divide the parts of the texts, I write the introduction, Sophia writes the main part, then I work on the conclusion". The student's comments seem to reflect the *divide and conquer* style proposed by Yim et al. (2017) where the writers write their own parts and rarely edit each other's text. However, this view contradicts the data obtained from the students' digital artefacts where Demetra's and Sophia's (G2) writing patterns were in line with the *cooperative revision* style (during the out-of-class activity) and the *main writer* style (during the in-class activity). The *main writer* style was particularly discussed because it was the predominant pattern observed during the in-class activity. Spyros, who states his preference to work face-to-face rather than through virtual communication, explains "[w]hen you work face-to-face, one has the ideas and the other writes them, because he or she is quicker with using the keyboard". This in turn, led to the script copyediting theme. Only Sophia and Demetra (G2) mentioned checking the final version of their text. The other groups, surprisingly, admitted not looking at it because as Pablo (G4 and G1) puts it, "we trust our peers".

The planning stages were also explored. Many participants reported on the use of different tools, such as Skype, Messenger, or Facebook closed groups, to discuss the ideas for the creation of their texts during the out-of-class activity. Aristos (G3) explained that "[s]omebody has an idea and shares it on Messenger, then the other looks for data or information, and then we start writing together". This division of work described by Aristos brings up the three forms of distributed constructionism proposed by Resnick (1996): (1) discussing constructions, as G3 did through Messenger; (2) sharing constructions, as they did when they shared the information they looked for; and (3) collaborating on constructions, when they worked on the creation of their digital artefacts.

The willingness to work in a group again was one of the items whose score decreased in the postQ. When asked about the reasons for this, different responses emerged:

> "It depends on the topic of the task. There are topics where you prefer to work alone rather than in groups" (Sophia, G2).

> "It depends on the people you work with" (Stavria, G1).

> "I always had problems with learning other languages so working in groups sometimes helps me but other times not" (Giason, G4).

Giason's statement led to the last topic examined during the interview: the improvement of language skills with collaborative writing activities. Interestingly, most of the students expressed feelings of doubtfulness with regards to the efficacy of collaborative writing practices in language learning, in Aristos' (G3) words "[f]or me it is the same, I don't feel I'm learning more in this way".

4. Conclusions

This study investigated students' attitudes towards digital artefact creation through collaborative writing in a Spanish for academic purposes class. It analysed students' asynchronous and synchronous collaborative writing practices and explored students' beliefs regarding collaborative writing with the use of technology. A worth mentioning conclusion relates to the group interaction patterns which differed between tasks: while for the out-of-class activity, assigned as an asynchronous collaborative writing task, there were a variety in writing patterns, mainly, the *main writer*, the *cooperative revision*, and the *synchronous hands-on* styles (Yim et al., 2017). The in-class activity presented the same pattern among the groups, that is, *main writer* and *synchronous hands-on* styles combined. Students' beliefs were also mediated by task type. The questionnaires' results showed that students perceived more positively their writing roles, sharing ideas and motivation for the out-of-class writing activity, and more negatively the planning stages, willingness to work in a group again, boosting confidence, and creative writing after the in-class writing activity. In line with the results obtained by Cho (2017), not only did task type influence students' perceptions, but also matches/mismatches between participants and students' self-perceived and other perceived roles have had an influence on shaping students' perceptions, as reported in the focus group interview.

Some limitations of the study should be acknowledged. First, the current study reports a small case research where only eight students participated. Future researchers may recruit a larger sample of participants to offer more robust claims. Secondly, results are solely based on two collaborative writing activities and students' perceptions related to those activities. Future research could benefit from designing a study where more collaborative writing activities are included. These limitations notwithstanding, generate ideas not only for future research but also for language instructors who may consider implementing collaborative writing activities that consider the students' attitudes and beliefs reported in this study, i.e. students' motivation and more active participation in an asynchronous, collaborative writing activity, and their reluctance to participate again in a collaborative writing experience after a synchronous task.

5. Supplementary materials

https://research-publishing.box.com/s/rsuozmqw60z16fph90t2wu0isgbinu5n

References

Cho, H. (2017). Synchronous web-based collaborative writing: factors mediating interaction among second-language writers. *Journal of Second Language Writing, 36*, 37-51. https://doi.org/10.1016/j.jslw.2017.05.013

Creswell, J. (2007). *Qualitative inquiry & research design*. Sage.

Duff, P. (2008). *Case study research in applied linguistics*. Laurance Erlbaum.

Dörney, Z. (2010). *Questionnaires in second language research*. Routledge.

Gökçe, I. (2001). *Effects of collaborative writing on attitudes of learners towards writing at Anadolu University preparatory school*. Unpublished PhD dissertation. Bilkent University, Ankara.

Kessler, G. (2013). Collaborative language learning in co-constructed participatory culture. *CALICO Journal, 30*(3), 307-322.

Larson-Hall, J. (2010). *A guide to doing statistics in second language research using SPSS*. Routledge. https://doi.org/10.4324/9780203875964

Miles, V. C., McCarthy, J. C., Dix, A. J., Harrison, M. D., & Monk, A. F. (1993). Reviewing designs for a synchronous-asynchronous group editing environment. In M. Sharples (Ed.), *Computer supported collaborative writing* (pp. 137-160). Springer-Verlag. https://doi.org/10.1007/978-1-4471-2007-0_8

Nespor, J. (2000). Anonymity and place in qualitative inquiry. *Qualitative Inquiry, 6*(4), 546-569. https://doi.org/10.1177/107780040000600408

Olson, J. S., Wang, D., Zhang, J., & Olson, G. M. (2017). How people write together now: beginning the investigation with advanced undergraduates in a project course. *ACM Transactions on Computer-Human Interaction (TOCHI), 24*(1). https://doi.org/10.1145/3038919

Papert, S. (1980). *Mindstorms: children, computers and powerful ideas*. Basic Books.

Papert, S. (1993). *The children's machine: rethinking school in the age of the computer*. Basic Books.

Papert, S., & Harel, I. (1991). Situating constructionism. En S. Papert & I. Harel (Eds), *Constructionism* (pp. 1-11). Ablex.

Parmaxi, A., & Zaphiris, P. (2015). Developing a framework for social technologies in learning via design-based research. *Educational Media International, 52*(1), 33-46. https://doi.org/10.1080/09523987.2015.1005424

Parmaxi, A., Zaphiris, P., & Ioannou, A. (2016) Enacting artifact-based activities for social technologies in language learning using a design-based research approach. *Computers in Human Behavior, 63*, 556-567. https://doi.org/10.1016/j.chb.2016.05.072

Resnick, M. (1996). Distributed constructionism. In D. C. Edelson & E. A. Domeshek (Eds), *Proceedings of the 1996 international conference on Learning sciences* (pp. 280-284). International Society of the Learning Sciences.

Reynolds, S., Wooley, B., & Wooley, T. (1911). *Seems So! A working-class view of politics*. Macmillan.

Rüschoff, B. (2004) Language. In H. Adelsherger, B. Collis & J. M. Pawlowski (Eds), *Handbook on information technologies for education and training* (pp. 523-539). Springer.

Rüschoff, B., & Ritter, M. (2001) Technology-enhanced language learning: construction of knowledge and template-based learning in the foreign language classroom. *Computer Assisted Language Learning, 14*(3-4), 219-232. https://doi.org/10.1076/call.14.3.219.5789

Sevilla-Pavón, A. (2015). Examining collective authorship in collaborative writing tasks through digital storytelling. *European Journal of Open, Distance and E-Learning, 18*(1).

Sharples, M. (1993). *Introduction*. In M. Sharples (Ed.), *Computer supported collaborative writing* (pp. 1-8). Springer-Verlag.

Wang, D., Olson, J. S., Zhang, J., Nguyen, T., & Olson, G. M. (2015a). How students collaboratively write using Google Docs. In *iConference 2015 Proceedings*.

Wang, D., Olson, J., Zhang, J., Nguyen, T., & Olson, G. (2015b). DocuViz: visualizing collaborative writing. In *CHI'15 Proceedings of the 33rd Annual ACM Conference on Human Factors in Computing Systems* (pp. 1865-1874). https://doi.org/10.1145/2702123.2702517

Yim, S., Wang, D., Olson, J., Vu, V., & Warschauer, M. (2017) Synchronous collaborative writing in the classroom: undergraduates' collaboration practices and their impact on writing style, quality, and quantity. In *CSCW'17 Proceedings of the 2017 ACM Conference on Computer Supported Cooperative Work and Social Computing* (pp. 468-479). https://doi.org/10.1145/2998181.2998356

Yim, S., & Warschauer, M. (2017). Web-based collaborative writing in L2 contexts: methodological insights from text mining. *Language Learning & Technology, 21*(1), 146-165.

4. The integration of assistive technologies in the SEN EAP classroom: raising awareness

Theodora Charalambous[1],
Salomi Papadima-Sophocleous[2],
and Christina Nicole Giannikas[3]

Abstract

Students with Special Educational Needs (SEN) in universities are a challenging issue of much concern. University students often need to attend English for Academic Purposes (EAP) classes to complete their studies, as it is necessary for their academic progress. According to Gathercole, Alloway, Willis, and Adams (2006), SEN students show low levels of working memory performance. Also, they are often diagnosed with poor concentration (Westwood, 2007), spelling difficulties (dysorthographia), and often have trouble understanding and applying phonic decoding principles (Westwood, 2007). When these struggling skills are not catered for properly they are often the cause for SEN EAP students falling behind in their studies as their lessons increase in their level of difficulty. Subsequently, it is important for these students, instead of being part of regular EAP classes where they may not receive the required attention, to be taught in a specialised learning environment with tools that will attend to their needs and facilitate the language learning process. Moreover, with the continuous growth of technology and the systematic training of educators in the use of technology, it has been widely acknowledged that technology can assist and benefit

---

1. Limassol, Cyprus; theodora.94ch@gmail.com; https://orcid.org/0000-0002-2599-1416

2. Cyprus University of Technology, Limassol, Cyprus; salomi.papadima@cut.ac.cy; https://orcid.org/0000-0003-4444-4882

3. Cyprus University of Technology, Limassol, Cyprus; christina.giannikas@cut.ac.cy; https://orcid.org/0000-0002-5653-6803

How to cite: Charalambous, T., Papadima-Sophocleous, S., & Giannikas, C. N. (2021). The integration of assistive technologies in the SEN EAP classroom: raising awareness. In S. Papadima-Sophocleous, E. Kakoulli Constantinou & C. N. Giannikas (Eds), *Tertiary education language learning: a collection of research* (pp. 65-88). Research-publishing.net. https://doi.org/10.14705/rpnet.2021.51.1255

Chapter 4

EAP practice in various ways. Based on students' needs analysis conducted by the instructor at the beginning of the course, the present study investigates the different Assistive Technologies (ATs) used by an SEN EAP instructor in order to support students' memorisation, concentration, and spelling. Furthermore, it investigates the SEN EAP students' attitudes towards the specialised EAP process. The aim of the present chapter is to raise awareness in the type of support given to university SEN EAP students with the use of ATs in SEN EAP contexts.

Keywords: SEN, CALL, EAP, language education, higher education, qualitative research, classroom-based research.

1. Introduction

SEN in higher education is a challenging issue that needs utmost attention. As SEN students move on to tertiary education they are often expected to take EAP and English for Specific Academic Purposes (ESAP) classes, where they often struggle with low levels of working memory performance (Gathercole et al., 2006), poor concentration (Westwood, 2007), dysorthographia, and often have severe difficulties with understanding and applying phonic decoding principles (Westwood, 2007). When these issues are not appropriately addressed, they are often the cause for SEN students losing all motivation and progress less in their English language development than they would have if their strengths and weaknesses were properly channelled. The present chapter sheds light on useful and meaningful practices in the area of SEN EAP with the use of ATs in higher education. This is done by sharing the students' and the instructor's experiences in the hope that it would fill some of the gap in the area of raising awareness of stakeholders, such as instructors, and policy makers. Cyprus University of Technology (CUT), where the research was conducted, is an example, among other universities, which has designed a personalised support programme with ATs, which are any devices, equipment, or product systems that increase, maintain, and/or improve the functional capabilities of SEN students (CUT Language Centre Language Policy, n.d.). The study was guided by two research questions, which derived from the purpose of the study.

- Which ATs are used by SEN EAP teachers in SEN EAP classes and how do the specific ATs improve SEN EAP students' memorisation, concentration, and spelling skills, and raise awareness in the area?

- Which are the students' attitudes towards these SEN EAP technology-supported classes, which raise awareness in the area from the students' perspective?

2. Literature review

2.1. Supporting SEN EAP/ESAP students

The last recommendation of the European Commission (2018) highlights quality education and learning to ensure opportunities to all students. Including SEN students in higher education, and assisting them throughout their academic journey, is something that has been promoted by many European universities. Among these universities is the University of Cyprus (UCY Legislation, n.d.) which supports students with learning difficulties and hearing or visual impairments. The aforementioned university includes audiovisual content in the lectures and uses supportive technology which assists these students to perform at their full capacity. Another example is the Masaryk University in the Czech Republic (Claeys-Kulik, Jørgensen, & Stöber, 2019) which has developed inclusive educational methods by implementing technological measures to make education, documents, and communication accessible to students with special needs. According to Broom (2017), the European Parliament Policy Department of Citizens' Rights and Constitutional Affairs mentioned that inclusive education has to recognise, accept, and respond to learners' diversity and prepare them to engage in society. As it was mentioned above, EAP courses are offered by universities in order to initiate students into the expectations of the academic world. In their study, Asaoka and Usui (2003) mention that this initiation cannot be achieved if practitioners are not aware of their students' learning needs. Language educators need to be aware of their students' previous knowledge, their experiences, and, most importantly, any possible difficulties they may face. For the purpose of the present research, the review was narrowed down to those often related to specific skills. For example, SEN students may struggle with their working memory, which is responsible for enabling the mind to store information in order to comprehend reading or planning a series of thoughts (Holmes & Gathercole, 2012). SEN students may suffer from Attention Deficit Hyperactivity Disorder (ADHD) or Attention Deficit Disorder (ADD); both are very common and can often lead SEN students to frustration and the inability to concentrate (Barrett, 2013). Spelling has also proven to be challenging and can interfere with the execution of other composing processes and writing development (Graham, 1999). In addition to this, English is considered to be an opaque language when it comes to orthography (Reason, 2004). Thus, the automaticity and fluency in the English language that EAP students should have, remains problematic to SEN students.

2.2. Supporting SEN EAP/ESAP students with the use of ATs

ATs have been evident in the field of education since 1988 when The Individuals with Disabilities Education Act (IDEA) was implemented in the USA. Thanks to IDEA, technological advances increased the potential of the integration of students with learning differences into general and inclusive education (Fein, 1996). According to Hasselbring and Glaser (2000), computer technology can highly assist and motivate students with both mild and severe difficulties to become active learners. Also as Perna, Varriale, and Ferrara (2020) argue that ATs can support and assist SEN students' full participation during their learning process, as they help students overcome the barriers created by traditional educational methods (Giannikas, 2020). The rapid growth of the usage of ATs has also offered a lot in teaching (Edyburn, 2004). Technology is highly utilised in the contemporary English as a Second Language (ESL) teaching processes. It is considered to be the most innovative endeavour, as it is proved that it motivates students, and improves the teaching methods and students' results

(Azmat, 2016). Young adult SEN ESL learners are immensely benefitted by the introduction of technology in their learning path as well, as they are considered to be 'digital natives' (Kosunen, 2016, p. 1). Different software and applications, aiming at enhancing SEN students' learning process, exist as researchers attempt to involve different aspects of technology to support SEN students' education (Loizides, Kartapanis, Sella, & Papadima-Sophocleous, 2015).

2.3. Previous research in higher education SEN EAP

The review in this area revealed that there is little research on higher education SEN EAP students' difficulties. In their paper, for example, Young, Schaefer, and Lesley (2019) argue that Japanese SEN students enrolled in higher education EAP classes were taught by instructors specifically trained for this framework, making their education more effective. However, ATs were not mentioned in the specific study. Another recent research related to the specific topic, carried out by Blázquez Arribas, Barros del Rio, Peñalver, and Sigona (2020), sheds light on the learning difficulties among adults who are learning English in higher education. The specific research suggests and highlights the use of technology in the classroom as it can contribute to the inclusion of students with difficulties and improve their learning process. More specifically, the study discusses the outcomes of the European project EN-ABILITIES (Enabling Inclusive Education through Technology). A large amount of research exists on SEN students in higher education. However, the difficulties that SEN students face in EAP classes that are offered in universities, and how ATs can be used to support these students, is a topic that needs to be further explored in order to raise awareness and improve SEN/EAP learning and teaching practices.

2.4. Awareness

Awareness is the "knowledge that something exists, or understanding of a situation or subject at the present time based on information or experience"[4].

---

4. https://dictionary.cambridge.org/dictionary/english/awareness

Chapter 4

According to Sayers (2006), awareness-raising, however, is a tool which stimulates discussions and innovations in the design of the process. To raise awareness is to inform and educate the wider public about a topic or issue with the intention of influencing attitudes, behaviours, and beliefs towards the achievement of a defined purpose or goal (Sayers, 2006). The present study concentrates on a SEN/EAP tertiary education programme. The aim is to raise awareness, in other words knowledge and understanding, of the integration of ATs in the SEN EAP classroom of stakeholders, such as ESL instructors and policy makers, by sharing data and the experiences of the participants' use of ATs in the SEN EAP programme.

3. Methodology

3.1. Participants

The research was carried out at the CUT Language Centre during the 2017, autumn semester. The participants were two classes of first year SEN EAP students, taught by the same specialised SEN EAP educator. Class A had three students and Class B four students. Students' average age was 19. For anonymity purposes, students were referred to as A1, A2, A3, B1, B2, B3, and B4. The students' profile was provided by the SEN EAP educator, who is an experienced English instructor specialised in SEN education. The two observed classes consisted of mixed abilities students who faced ADD, ADHD, mild and severe dyslexia, and dysorthographia. More specifically, students A1, A2, and A3 were facing severe dyslexia and generally, as the SEN EAP educator mentioned, they were weak students, who were also struggling with technology. Students B1, B3, and B4 were facing mild dyslexia combined with ADHD. Lastly, student B2 had dysorthographia combined with ADD. The participants were Cypriots and Greek native speakers.

The instructor was also considered a participant of the study and was observed and interviewed as well, thus enriching the research data. The specific course observed, aiming to provide meaningful EAP lessons to these students, as EAP is a mandatory module at CUT. According to the specific university, the EAP course prepares and equips students with the language skills that are needed to successfully carry out their studies and research. Additionally, it prepares them for their future academic and professional careers (CUT Language Centre Language Policy, n.d.).

3.2. Research approach

The research studied the nature of SEN EAP classrooms and the use of ATs. Classroom observations were conducted to facilitate the process of the naturalistic inquiry known as the research method that best serves the social and the behavioural sciences (Guba & Lincoln, 1982). According to Lincoln (2007), the naturalistic inquiry is an interpretive and non-experimental research which creates a meaningful reality when dealing with human research. This was used as the basis of this research. Qualitative research builds a complex out of words, and reports detailed views in a natural setting (Sogunro, 2002). Thus, the qualitative research methodologies were used to collect the necessary in-class data.

3.3. Data collection tools

Three different tools were used for data collection: observation, reflective journal, and interviews. A detailed description of the function of these tools follows in the next sections.

3.3.1. Observation

An observation protocol was completed by Researcher 1 during the observations. Nine scheduled observations were carried out in total: five with the first group and four with the second. The observation protocol was used in order to record the ATs that were being used during the lessons. Moreover, the protocol was used to record the skills that were being benefitted by each of the ATs used. Finally, the students' attitudes and difficulties, the teacher's challenges, and the objectives of the lesson were also recorded.

3.3.2. *Reflective journal*

A reflective journal, which recognises the multiple realities existing around the topic, was completed by Researcher 1 at the end of each observation. It is a record of the researcher's experiences, thoughts, and feelings after observing each lesson. Keeping a journal led Researcher 1 to a better understanding (Rogers et al., 2018) of the SEN EAP teaching and learning of the specific case and the use of ATs.

3.3.3. *Interviews*

Finally, in order to strengthen the qualitative nature of the research and to ensure the validity and the reliability of the journal, the data were triangulated with the use of a third data collection tool, the interviews. This included a semi-structured interview for the instructor, and structured interviews for the students. The interviews were carried out when the nine observations were completed. All of the interviews were held after the final observation. They were conducted with each participant individually. They were recorded and later transcribed verbatim. All participants were interviewed individually in order to ensure the quality and the confidentiality of the interviews. The students' structured interview included six open-ended and leading types of questions. The students were asked about their level in English. They were also asked to identify and share their weaknesses considering English language learning. They were also asked if they find the SEN EAP course a useful course for their academic studies. The final question was whether they find technologically assisted English lessons better than the mainstream English languages lessons where traditional methods are used.

3.4. Data analysis

Due to the qualitative nature of the research and the small number of participants, it was decided not to use any qualitative data analysis software for the data analysis. Also, it was possible that a qualitative data analysis software would dehumanise the data, distance the researcher, and, therefore, the complexity and the richness of it could be lost (John & Johnson, 2000). In order to maintain a close relationship between the researchers and the data, the data analysis was carried out manually. According to Webb (1999), the manual approach is recommended for small-scale studies in order to gain insight into the intuitive aspects of the analysis.

The next step was to choose the methods with which the data for each question would be analysed.

The method chosen for the analysis of Question 1 was the *narrative analysis*. More specifically, the data were analysed by combining two different approaches to conduct a narrative analysis:

- the *thematic analysis*, which focuses on 'what' is said according to the content of the text (Riessman & Quinney, 2005); and

- the *structural analysis*, which focuses on 'how' things happened by creating a brief, topically-centred narrative based on an abstract summary of the story, that focuses on the place, the characters, and the situation (Riessman & Quinney, 2005).

According to Patton and Cochran (2002), thematic analysis is the method that identifies the common issues that recur across the data. Another data analysis method is structural analysis, which has an intention to extrapolate and understand better specific personal experiences (Bamberg, 2012). In the present research, both of the methods were used. The first one was used in order to identify the different ATs used and the skills that each one of them benefitted. The latter was used to present the way that the specific ATs benefitted the identified skill, according to the observations and the reflective journal. The combination of these two methods of data analysis and the accumulation of the data aimed to raise the awareness of SEN, SEN ESL, and SEN EAP educators who need to use more ATs in their teaching methods.

Narrative analysis was also chosen for Question 2. The students' attitudes expressed during their interviews were summarised in order to reach the point

Chapter 4

of their story (Riessman & Quinney, 2005). For Question 2, narrative analysis was conducted through structural analysis which, as already mentioned, creates an abstract of the story.

4. Discussion of the findings

4.1. Discussion of the data for Question 1

In order to raise awareness of the integration of ATs in an SEN EAP classroom, the following data were recorded: the ATs used by the SEN EAP teacher in the SEN EAP class; the way they were used to improve SEN EAP students' memorisation, concentration, and spelling skills. Thematic Analysis was chosen to identify the different ATs used and the skill that each one of them benefitted. By accumulating the information derived from the data and focusing on 'what' was said according to the content, an abstract was first created where a lot of ATs were noted down as frequently used in the SEN EAP classes observed. The ATs that were used to benefit the students were the ones presented below, starting from the most frequently used:

- projector;
- Google Drive (cloud storage) https://www.google.com/drive/;
- mobile phones;
- computers/laptops;
- PowerPoint/Google Slides https://office.live.com/start/powerpoint.aspx, https://www.google.com/slides/about/;
- Kahoot (online game-based learning platform) https://kahoot.com/;
- Quizlet (online study application) https://quizlet.com/;
- Youtube videos https://www.youtube.com/;
- headphones;
- Google search https://www.google.com/;
- e-library (CUT) https://library.cut.ac.cy/;
- Glogster (online interactive learning tool) http://edu.glogster.com/;
- Smartdraw (online diagramming tool) https://www.smartdraw.com/;

- QR codes & QR Code Reader application.

Through the observations and semi-structured interview with the SEN EAP instructor, the three struggling skills (spelling, memorisation, and concentration) that improved due to ATs were observed and discussed. The findings are presented in Table 1.

Table 1. Skills benefitted by the devices and ATs used

	Spelling	Memorisation	Concentration
Projector		✓	✓
Google Drive		✓	
Mobile Phones			✓
Computers/Laptops			✓
PowerPoint/Google Slides	✓	✓	
Kahoot		✓	✓
Quizlet	✓	✓	✓
Youtube Videos		✓	✓
Headphones			
Google search		✓	✓
E-library (CUT)		✓	✓
Glogster		✓	✓
Smartdraw		✓	✓
QR Codes & QR Code Reader Application		✓	

The way the specific ATs benefitted the identified skill was analysed through the structural analysis process, as described earlier. The observations and the reflective journal were used to document what was happening during the lesson and how the students were assisted by the ATs used. More specifically, the lessons were observed and later the interpretation of whether the ATs used benefitted and kept the students concentrated was transferred to the reflective journal. Moreover, the researcher observed whether the students were productive and whether their memorisation and spelling skills were benefitted in any way by the presence of the ATs. Finally, the researcher observed whether there were any positive or negative comments by the students about the ATs used. The intention

Chapter 4

was to better understand the participants' experiences of the integration of ATs in the SEN EAP class.

What the instructor said about the benefits of the projector in SEN EAP classes was:

> "I believe that using technology and audiovisual technology can be beneficial to any kind of students but mainly with these students who face difficulties with memory and concentration".

It was noted that the **projector** was the most frequently used tool during the lessons, as it was used during all of the observations. More specifically, according to the data collected, students' concentration was reinforced by the use of the projector as it helped them to follow the flow of the class. In this way, memorisation, which is closely linked to concentration, was benefitted at the same time.

All the students of SEN EAP classes had full access, in **Google Drive,** to the shared material, presentations, and notes prepared by the teacher during the whole semester. In this way, students could easily access all material from any device anytime, and were able to study and revise autonomously in order to memorise and refresh the material they were taught. As the instructor also mentioned, Google Drive is highly used in order to help students remember concepts and ideas.

According to the checklist and the observations, **mobile phones** and **laptops** were technologies used in class that were benefiting SEN EAP students' concentration. According to the instructor:

> "They actually use their own devices, their mobile phones, which they are familiar with, and they believe that they own the activity, that they feel this ownership, independence and autonomy".

The permission to use their own devices as a tool for learning and revising made the process more personal for them, making them feel more comfortable and motivated. Thus, one could argue that their concentration was empowered, as their interest about the task and the material increased.

PowerPoint/Google Slides allowed students to create hands-on presentations; the skills which were observed to be practised when students were asked to carry out a presentation were spelling and memorisation. In the observation protocols and the journal, it was noted that some presentations carried out by the students did not have any spelling mistakes and the students memorised the content of their project before introducing it. Spelling was benefitted as the composition of a presentation required practising writing by students, and they had to recall from memory how to write down the words and terms that they had learnt. Also, autocorrection, which is provided by PowerPoint/Google Slides, reminded them how some of the words are written correctly. Furthermore, students' skill of memorisation was assisted as the hands-on tasks they were requested to carry out with the use of PowerPoint/Google Slides required from them to recall all the memorised input they gained during SEN EAP classes.

Kahoot was highly popular among the students observed. According to the instructor, it is an extremely successful application which has the nature of a game and it also includes competition among them, which is another motivation. It was also mentioned that the music and the visuals it includes and the fact that they need to use their own device are factors that lead to concentration. Another thing that was mentioned and observed about Kahoot was that it helped them practise at their own pace, and be self-corrected, and practise again and again as many times they want in order to achieve their goal, which is learning their vocabulary; memorisation was also empowered.

Quizlet was observed to be highly used for revising and practising purposes during the lessons. As the instructor supported Quizlet, apart from helping them to memorise and remember new vocabulary in the target language, it actually helped them to stay concentrated for a long time on the new language. It was also mentioned that the application corrects misspelled words which they can listen to letter by letter and see the correct form of the word. In this way, they can be self-corrected and self-taught.

By using **YouTube videos** during the lessons, the skill of memorisation and concentration was assisted as this tool was often used to introduce new vocabulary. According to the instructor, videos are combining audiovisual material that helps students save material because they have linked it with audio and visual information. Also, it was mentioned by the instructor, that videos enable them to actually remember what they have learnt before, allowing students can recall specific information. So, by combining audiovisual material this helped students remember it easier. Moreover, YouTube was also used as a revising tool, as videos often provided students with information and they had to connect that with what they had learnt before.

Headphones enhanced students' concentration as they kept students focused on their listening tasks without being distracted by the rest of the group. The personal headphones that students used were linked to their personal computers giving them the opportunity to pause and replay the audio as many times as it was needed. The autonomicity that headphones provided to students increased their levels of *concentration*. All students were trying their best. This was recorded in the observation notes.

It was also observed in one of the lessons that students were encouraged to use and explore **Google search** for various tasks, such as research and translation. This activity required students' concentration, and the permission to use Google search autonomously from their smartphones or the computers in order to carry out searches and find information for different kinds of activities, motivated them to stay focused. Memorisation was benefitted as well when they had to use Google search autonomously to find and access different electronic sources, as they had to recall from memory different kinds of terms they had learnt in L2 in order to use them and recognise them.

As higher education students, the students had to familiarise themselves with the use of the **CUT e-library**. It was observed that this technology triggered their skills of concentration and memorisation as the gap filling with the keywords needed to be done carefully, and students had to scan through the content thoroughly to find what would be useful for them.

Glogster was another software with interactive features that was included in the teaching and learning process. It was used by the instructor to enhance students in their concentration and memorisation. The instructor mentioned that it is a tool that combines words with visuals, and it can gather all the information on a subject in one interactive picture, increasing students' concentration, and subsequently triggering their memorisation skill.

Smartdraw, which was recorded in the observation notes, was used by the teacher in class in order to empower students' concentration and memorisation. This online diagramming tool combines words with visuals, like Glogster, and the material becomes more informative and eye-catching to students. In this way, as it was observed when the specific tool was used in class, students were able to concentrate and memorise better what they were taught as their interest was triggered.

Finally, **QR codes & the QR Code Reader application** triggered the SEN EAP students' skill of memorisation. This tool was observed to be used by the SEN EAP teacher in order to introduce or revise new vocabulary. The instructor supported that students found this AT quite interesting and different. This playful way, as both the students and the instructor referred to, of interacting with the new language was contributing to their better memorisation of the new input.

The data analysis revealed that there were a lot of ATs integrated in the SEN EAP programme that helped in improving spelling, memorisation, and concentration. It also revealed the way the specific ATs improved the identified skills. The sharing of this practice and the results of this research may prove useful in raising awareness of the potential of technology integration in SEN EAP programmes.

4.2. Discussion of the data for Question 2

Another aspect that was researched in order to raise awareness of the usefulness of the integration of ATs in SEN EAP programmes was the study of the students' attitudes of these SEN EAP technology-supported classes. The pie chart in Figure 1 presents the general attitudes of the seven students towards the SEN EAP ATs supported classes. The answers derived from the data collected from

Chapter 4

the semi-structured interview, the observations, and the reflective journal. They were analysed with the use of narrative and structural analysis. Their attitudes were divided into negative, positive, and neutral. According to the data, the SEAN EAP students who participated in the research were separated into two SEN EAP classes: one with three students and one with four, the three-student group was referred to as Group A and the four-student group as Group B.

Figure 1. Students' attitude towards SEN EAP classes (N=4)

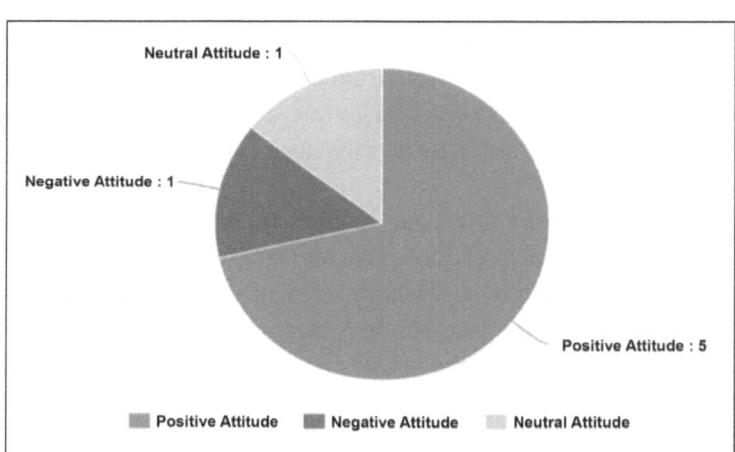

As presented in Figure 1, the majority of the students (five students out of seven) had a positive attitude towards the SEN EAP technology enhanced classes.

- Positive attitude

As mentioned before, students were asked some questions and their answers were summarised in order to interpret their attitudes. Some of the questions and the summaries of their answers are presented below.

> "Do you consider the English Lesson offered by your university to students with learning difficulties, a useful lesson? If yes, why? If not, why?"

For the question above, five out of seven students (A1, A2, A3, B3, and B4), who had a positive attitude towards SEN EAP classes, characterised the lessons as **useful** and **alternative**, especially designed for the kind of students who were used to inclusive classes, where their difficulties were neglected or not **sufficiently** supported. It was also mentioned by student B3 that the SEN EAP instructor was able to focus more on each student as the size of the class was small. Student A2 stated that the extra support given by the instructor and the small size of the class gave students the **confidence** that the lessons were not going to be as hard as they would be in a regular EAP class.

> "Do you find technologically assisted English language learning more helpful than the traditional methods of learning that your teachers have been using in the past? If yes, how did the current method help you?"

For this question, five out of seven SEN EAP students (A1, A2, A3, B3, and B4), who had a positive attitude, stated that technologically assisted English language learning is an **alternative** and more **helpful** method to the traditional use of coursebooks. According to the participants, this method helped them **overcome** the difficulties they face with learning. Students supported that the **new approaches** used, like the internet and games, assisted them in ways that traditional methods could not. As they mentioned, the specific SEN EAP classes have helped them **overcome** some struggling skills and contributed to effective English language learning.

In order to investigate why the majority of the students had a positive attitude, data from the Reflective Journal was summarised as well. According to the Reflective Journal data, the majority of the students were **more engaged** when they were asked to use their own mobile phones and compete with each other on the online assessing game, 'Kahoot'. Using their own mobile phones gave them **confidence** because it was a familiar device to them. The data showed that students felt that the classroom was a **safe environment**, which allowed them to feel more **comfortable** and **motivated**. As a result, they **concentrated more** and at the end of the lessons they were documented feeling satisfied. Also, the

Chapter 4

use of interesting YouTube videos with nice pictures and music kept them more **concentrated** and they were **encouraged** to work.

- Negative attitude

There was only one participant who had a negative attitude towards AT, according to the following responses.

> "Do you consider the English Lesson offered by your university to students with learning difficulties a useful lesson? If yes, why? If not, why?"

In contrast to the majority of students who had a positive attitude towards the SEN EAP classes, the student who had a negative attitude characterised these classes as **discomforting** and **unhelpful.**

> "Do you find the technologically assisted English language learning more helpful than the traditional methods of learning that your teachers have been using in the past? If yes, how did the current method help you?"

Student B2 stated that the lessons were not useful and that they **did not help** in any way. The methodology, the technology, and the games used in this class were characterised as **discomforting**.

Some negative feelings during the observations were also noted in the Reflective Journal. For example, when the students were asked to present a PowerPoint that they had created, there was a feeling that some of them felt **out of their comfort zone** and anxious, as they were making comments continuously about the **difficulties** they were facing both with the ATs and the language. Also, regarding Kahoot, there were two negative comments by student B2 who stated that the activities were **childish** and **unnecessary.**

- Neutral attitude

> "Do you consider the English Lesson offered by your university to students with learning difficulties a useful lesson? If yes, why? If not, why?"

Student B1 stated that they **benefitted** SEN students. However, Student B1 believed that the SEN EAP classes should be **optional,** as this kind of **exemption** may be **uncomfortable** and some students may have the fear of being **stigmatised** by the rest of the students who follow an EAP and not a SEN EAP class.

> "Do you find the technologically assisted English language learning more helpful than the traditional methods of learning that your teachers have been using in the past? If yes, how did the current method help you?"

According to the data, both methods can be **useful.** However, Student B1 stated:

> "I would say that, even though we are using a lot of technologies, the lesson remains a lesson. It is much more interactive and intense, but sometimes I find it foolish and there are a lot of technical problems".

According to the information gathered through the second question, the majority of students had a positive attitude towards SEN EAP classes and the methods used. This information can be used to raise awareness about how these differentiated courses and methods are perceived by SEN EAP students.

4.3. Limitations

The present research is not without limitations. It is important to mention that this is a small-scale study and the sample size of the students and the instructor observed was very small. The observation of more SEN EAP technology-supported classes can provide more, or even different, results. Furthermore, the integration of more ATs that can boost SEN EAP students' memorisation, concentration, and spelling skills even more is worth exploring. A larger sample size of students would reveal more attitudes that students may have towards

SEN EAP classes supported by ATs. A larger sample of students and SEN EAP educators could provide more information which will help raise awareness on the specific issue.

5. Conclusion

In conclusion, the present study has several positive outcomes. Firstly, a satisfying amount of devices and ATs proved to benefit the most common struggling skills of SEN EAP students in various ways. The data showed that almost all devices and ATs used assisted students with more than one of their struggling skills. The audiovisual nature of the ATs triggered the struggling skills of these students in order to support their performance to their full capacity. The devices and ATs mentioned in this study can be productively used by SEN EAP educators and generally all educators of SEN students in order to assist their students who are facing difficulties with spelling, memorisation, and concentration, as well as through research. Awareness is also raised on how important it is to include technology in language education that takes place in the tertiary sector.

Moreover, the present study gives a voice to SEN EAP students. This occurred through the interviews, where they expressed their opinion about the differentiated SEN EAP courses that were designed for them, including various devices and ATs to support them. The majority of SEN EAP students felt they benefitted from the specific classes as they found them useful, more sufficient to their needs, and they felt that they could succeed in overcoming their difficulties. However, there were a few arguments against SEN EAP, describing them as unnecessary or as classes that carry out the same outcomes with inclusive SEN EAP courses. These arguments focused on the classes themselves, though, and not the technology included.

Technological devices and ATs can be vital when teaching SEN students and integrating them in lessons. The teaching process can be channelled to students much more productively and effectively. For this reason, devices and ATs should be an integral component of SEN EAP courses, as EAP is highly important to be taught effectively to all higher education students since they need EAP to cope with their academic obligations.

Finally, SEN EAP classes may not be a first choice for students, however the data showed that with the right tools, SEN EAP classes enhanced students' learning and they should be included in the curriculum of higher education institutions. Through this study, it is expected that awareness will be raised about the importance of such classes, in order to motivate even the most reluctant SEN EAP students to participate and be benefitted by these specially designed courses and the ATs used. The present chapter sheds light on an under-researched area and current practices in SEN EAP with the use of ATs in higher education. This was done by sharing the students' and the instructor's experiences in the hope that it would fill some of the gap in the area of raising awareness of stakeholders, such as instructors and policy makers.

6. Acknowledgements

We would like to thank the CUT Language Centre SEN EAP students and their instructor for making this study possible.

References

Asaoka, C., & Usui, Y. (2003). Students' perceived problems in an EAP writing course. *JALT Journal, 25*(2), 143-172. https://doi.org/10.37546/jaltjj25.2-2

Azmat, Z. (2016). Using multimedia technology in ESL classroom: a case study of undergraduate students of English language at Aligarh Muslim University, Aligarh. *RJELAL Journal, 4*(2), 816-822.

Bamberg, M. (2012). Narrative analysis. In H. Cooper, P. M. Camic, D. L. Long, A. T. Panter, D. Rindskopf, & K. J. Sher (Eds), *APA handbook of research methods in psychology (vol 2). Research designs: quantitative, qualitative, neuropsychological, and biological* (pp. 85-102). American Psychological Association. https://doi.org/10.1037/13620-006

Barrett, B. (2013). Enabling students with disabilities with computing interaction and empowerment through enhanced strategic instructional course design. *Electronic Journal of Information Systems Evaluation, 16*(3), 164-173.

Blázquez Arribas, L., Barros del Río, M. A., Alcalde Peñalver, E., & Sigona, C. M. (2020). Teaching English to adults with disabilities: a digital solution through EN-ABILITIES. *Teaching English with Technology, 20*(1), 80-103.

Broom, D. M. (2017). *Policy department C citizens' rights and constitutional affairs*. Directorate General for Internal Policies, European Parliament.

Claeys-Kulik, A. L., Jørgensen, T. E., & Stöber, H. (2019). *Diversity, equity and inclusion in European higher education institutions: results from the INVITED project*. European University Association.

CUT Language Centre Language Policy (n.d.). https://www.cut.ac.cy/faculties/languagecentre/the-department/language-policy/?languageId=1

Edyburn, D. L. (2004). Rethinking assistive technology. *Special Education Technology Practice, 5*(4), 16-23.

European Commission. (2018). *Proposal for a council recommendation on promoting common values, inclusive education, and the European dimension of teaching*. https://ec.europa.eu/transparency/regdoc/rep/1/2018/EN/COM-2018-23-F1-EN-MAIN-PART-1.PDF

Fein, J. (1996). A history of legislative support for assistive technology. *Journal of Special Education Technology, 13*(1), 1-3.

Gathercole, S. E., Alloway, T. P., Willis, C., & Adams, A. M. (2006). Working memory in children with reading disabilities. *Journal of experimental child psychology, 93*(3), 265-281. https://doi.org/10.1016/j.jecp.2005.08.003

Giannikas, C. N. (2020). Technology and dyslexia: the path to effective language learning. *The Teacher Trainer Journal, 34*(3).

Graham, S. (1999). The role of text production skills in writing development: a special issue-I. *Learning Disability Quarterly, 22*(2), 75-77. https://doi.org/10.2307/1511267

Guba, E. G., & Lincoln, Y. S. (1982). Epistemological and methodological bases of naturalistic inquiry. *ECTJ, 30*(4), 233-252.

Hasselbring, T. S., & Glaser, C. H. W. (2000). Use of computer technology to help students with special needs. *The Future of Children, 10*(2). 102-122. https://doi.org/10.2307/1602691

Holmes, J., & Gathercole, S. E. (2012). Taking working memory training from the laboratory into schools. *Educational Psychology, 34*(4), 440-450. https://doi.org/10.1080/01443410.2013.797338

John, W. S., & Johnson, P. (2000). The pros and cons of data analysis software for qualitative research. *Journal of nursing scholarship, 32*(4), 393-397. https://doi.org/10.1111/j.1547-5069.2000.00393.x

Kosunen, K. (2016). *Adult language learning: using mini games to teach vocabulary in the ESL classroom.* http://urn.kb.se/resolve?urn=urn:nbn:se:his:diva-13103

Lincoln, Y. S. (2007). *Naturalistic inquiry.* The Blackwell encyclopedia of sociology.

Loizides, F., Kartapanis, I., Sella, F., & Papadima-Sophocleous, S. (2015). Mi. LA: multilingual and multifaceted mobile interactive applications for children with autism. In F. Helm, L. Bradley, M. Guarda & S. Thouësny (Eds), *Critical CALL – Proceedings of the 2015 EUROCALL Conference, Padova, Italy* (pp. 368-374). Research-publishing.net. https://doi.org/10.14705/rpnet.2015.000360

Patton, M. Q., & Cochran, M. (2002). *A guide to using qualitative research methodology.* Médecins Sans Frontières. https://evaluation.msf.org/sites/evaluation/files/a_guide_to_using_qualitative_research_methodology.pdf

Perna, G., Varriale, L., & Ferrara, M. (2020). Assistive technology for the social inclusion at school: a portrait of Italy. In Y. Baghdadi, A. Harfouche & M. Musso (Eds), *ICT for an inclusive world* (pp. 161-176). Springer. https://doi.org/10.1007/978-3-030-34269-2_13

Reason, R. (2004). Dyslexia in different languages: cross-linguistic comparisons. *British Journal of Educational Psychology, 74*, 486-487.

Riessman, C. K., & Quinney, L. (2005). Narrative in social work: a critical review. *Qualitative Social Work, 4*(4), 391-412. https://doi.org/10.1177/1473325005058643

Rogers, G. D., Mey, A., Chan, P. C., Lombard, M., & Miller, F. (2018). Development and validation of the Griffith University affective learning scale (GUALS): a tool for assessing affective learning in health professional students' reflective journals. *MedEdPublish*, 7(1). https://doi.org/10.15694/mep.2018.000002.1

Sayers, R. (2006). *Awareness-raising awareness-raising principles for information literacy, a case study.* Communication and Information (CI) UNESCO Asia and Pacific Regional Bureau for Education.

Sogunro, O. A. (2002). Selecting a quantitative or qualitative research methodology: an experience. Educational Research *Quarterly, 26*(1), 3-10.

UCY Legislation. (n.d.). University of Cyprus policy for quality assurance in teaching. https://www.ucy.ac.cy/graduateschool/documents/Phd/ENGLISH_QualityofTeachingPolicyDocument.pdf

Webb, C. (1999). Analysing qualitative data: computerized and other approaches. *Journal of advanced nursing, 29*(2), 323-330. https://doi.org/10.1046/j.1365-2648.1999.00892.x

Westwood, P. (2007). *Commonsense methods for children with special educational needs.* Routledge.

Young, D., Schaefer, M. Y., & Lesley, J. (2019). Accommodating students with disabilities studying English as a foreign language (practice brief). *Journal of Postsecondary Education and Disability, 32*(3), 311-319.

5. Professional development in English for specific purposes: designing the curriculum of an online ESP teacher education course

Elis Kakoulli Constantinou[1] and Salomi Papadima-Sophocleous[2]

Abstract

Despite the developments in the English for Specific Purposes (ESP) field, the field of ESP Teacher Education (TE) remains neglected. Research in the area of ESP TE has not been given much attention, and the opportunities ESP practitioners have for Professional Development (PD) are very limited. This chapter describes the development of a curriculum for an online ESP TE course, the ReTEESP Online. The process occurred in the context of a Technical Action Research (TAR) study, the purpose of which was to address the needs of a group of 24 language instructors in terms of ESP TE. The course was based on a literature review in ESP and ESP TE, including learning theories and TE models, and recent developments in curriculum design. The course was also informed by an analysis of the 24 language instructors' needs in ESP TE and a pilot implementation of the course.

Keywords: English for specific purposes, teacher education, professional development, curriculum development, needs analysis, cloud technologies, social constructivism, connectivism.

---

1. Cyprus University of Technology, Limassol, Cyprus; elis.constantinou@cut.ac.cy; https://orcid.org/0000-0001-8854-3816

2. Cyprus University of Technology, Limassol, Cyprus; salomi.papadima@cut.ac.cy; https://orcid.org/0000-0003-4444-4482

How to cite: Kakoulli Constantinou, E., & Papadima-Sophocleous, S. (2021). Professional development in English for specific purposes: designing the curriculum of an online ESP teacher education course. In S. Papadima-Sophocleous, E. Kakoulli Constantinou & C. N. Giannikas (Eds), *Tertiary education language learning: a collection of research* (pp. 89-109). Research-publishing.net. https://doi.org/10.14705/rpnet.2021.51.1256

Chapter 5

1. Introduction

In recent years, ESP has developed immensely; rapid internationalisation along with the predominance of English as a global language resulted in an increase in the numbers of students attending ESP courses. Due to the fact that ESP by definition focuses on the use of language for specialised purposes, there are many parameters that ESP practitioners need to take into consideration, which makes teaching ESP more challenging than teaching General English (GE). Therefore, ESP TE is more than necessary these days, and this intense need is expressed in the literature from different parts of the world (Abedeen, 2015; Basturkmen, 2010; Bezukladnikov & Kruze, 2012; Bracaj, 2014; Chen, 2012; Mahapatra, 2011). Nevertheless, research in the area of ESP TE has not been given enough attention, and the opportunities ESP practitioners have for PD are limited.

This chapter addresses the need for ESP TE. It describes the development of the curriculum for the ReTEESP Online, an Online Reflective TE course in ESP. The course was developed in the context of a TAR study; its purpose was to address the need of a group of 24 language instructors coming from different educational backgrounds in terms of ESP TE. The course was based on a literature review in ESP and ESP TE, including learning theories and TE models, developments in the field of curriculum design, an analysis of the 24 language instructors' needs in ESP TE, and a pilot implementation of the course.

2. The theoretical background of the ReTEESP Online

Following Richards and Farrell (2005), who support that TE processes derive from an amalgamation of different assumptions on how teachers learn, this study embraces the view that ESP TE could be founded on a comprehensive review of different processes that carry implications on the things that ESP practitioners' need to learn and the ways they could learn them. Such a review may involve the following: (1) research in ESP, (2) theories of learning, (3) TE models that resulted from theories of learning, including online TE, (4) suggestions for

ESP TE, and (5) recent developments in curriculum design. The subsections which follow briefly summarise the most important principles drawn from these aspects, which constitute the theoretical background of the ReTEESP Online.

2.1. Reviewing research in ESP

ESP emerged in the 1960s in an era of socioeconomic turbulence with growing numbers of university students, due to developments in science, business, and technology and an increasing number of migrants (Dudley-Evans & St John, 1998; Richards, 2001). ESP, as its name denotes, has a specialised nature. As Hutchinson and Waters (1987, p. 18) support, this does not refer to 'specialised varieties' of English, but rather to the different purposes for which the language might be used. Amongst the most important aspects of ESP are: (1) needs analysis, which is perhaps one of the foundations which ESP course design is based on (Belcher, 2009; Dudley-Evans & St John, 1998; Johns & Makalela, 2011; Flowerdew, 2013), (2) authenticity of material and tasks, which occupies a central role in ESP, even though it is a concept very often found in literature on language teaching in general (Benavent & Penamaria, 2011), and (3) the multifaceted and multidimensional role of the ESP practitioner (Dudley-Evans & St John, 1998; Johns, 2013).

Today ESP is thriving with more research studies being conducted in the field, more publications being released every year, and more ESP professional associations being established. Even though in the past, research in ESP related to genre and corpus studies, some of the topics that interest researchers in the ESP field nowadays deal with specific disciplines such as Business English (Alousque, 2016), students' acquisition of employability skills (Álvarez-Mayo, Gallagher-Brett, & Michel, 2017), and the integration of new technologies in ESP (Selevičienė, 2020).

ESP TE needs to revolve around all the principles and specialised processes of ESP, and inform the practitioners on the latest developments in the field, including the release of new research, the existence of different professional organisations, and the organisation of various events in the field. This was the basis on which the content of the ReTEESP Online was built.

2.2. Looking at theories of learning and TE models

As far as learning theories are concerned, which have an important impact on how teaching is achieved, two of the most influential theories of learning emerging in the last decades are social constructivism (Vygotsky, 1978) and connectivism (Siemens, 2005). According to social constructivism, individuals construct knowledge through the interaction of their past experiences and what they already know and the ideas, experiences, and activities with which they come in contact, in other words their social surroundings (Richardson, 1997). Learning is achieved through social interaction, and students learn best when they collaborate and when they are engaged in problem-solving situations. In this sense, knowledge is actively constructed and not passively received. Connectivism, relies on technology and networking for the discovery of knowledge. For Siemens (2005), knowledge exists in networks, and the key to finding knowledge is knowing to which network one has to look for it. Both of these approaches to learning denote that learning occurs where there is communication, interaction, exchange of ideas, and collaboration.

Social constructivist and connectivist approaches to leaning influenced the development of current TE models. The two theories of learning are connected with the evolvement of the reflective model for TE, a sociocultural perspective to TE, and the development of critical language TE, which influenced the TE field. Firstly, the reflective model for TE (Wallace, 1991, p. 14), which was based on constructivist approaches to learning and experiential learning, suggests that the teachers acquire two types of knowledge; the received knowledge, which involves all the 'intellectual content' received, and the experiential knowledge, which relates to knowledge acquired through experience and reflection. Through putting into practice the knowledge they acquire and through reflection on practice, teachers manage to reach professional competence. This TE model favours a 'practising what you preach' approach, in other words, the belief that every teacher training programme should reflect in its practice all the theories and approaches that it wishes to convey to the trainees (Wallace, 1991, pp. 18-20). Another TE approach, the sociocultural perspective to TE, is rooted in the social constructivist and connectivist theories of learning, emphasising the value of professional networks. This perspective to TE was realised through the development of communities of practice (Wenger, 1998), which are formed by people who are learning together as part of a professional network. These professional networks usually operate online. Finally, another TE model, which is becoming popular nowadays, is that of critical language TE, which stems from critical pedagogy, concerned with social action and educational change, the results of global migration and social diversity (Hawkins & Norton, 2009). This TE model promotes the ideas of social equality and justice.

Following these developments in the area of learning in general, and TE in particular, ESP TE can adopt an inclusive approach that combines elements from all these current TE models, as suggested by Maggioli (2012). This idea was followed in the design of the ReTEESP Online, which was founded on social constructivism and connectivism and inspired by all TE models discussed in this section.

2.3. Considering online TE

Developments in the areas of learning and TE have led to the emergence of online learning and online TE (Dede, 2006). Researchers in the field emphasise the significance of teacher learning online built on sound pedagogical foundations; Henry and Meadows (2008), Maggioli (2012), and Powell and Bodur (2019) suggest principles through which online TE can be efficient. Some of the most important principles of online TE, as they were expressed by these researchers, involved the following realisations:

- online learning is different than regular classroom learning, therefore special adjustments need to be made, and constant and detailed guidance must be provided to the teachers;

- learning must be informed by pedagogy and teachers must engage in meaningful activities and interaction;

- teachers need to have a sense of presence and interaction with other colleagues and the facilitator, whom they need to perceive as real people;

Chapter 5

- technology is only a tool; and

- assessment needs to be ongoing.

These principles are important in online TE, and were considered in the design of the ReTEESP Online.

2.4. Reviewing research in ESP TE

A review of the literature in the field of ESP TE, starting from 1983 with Ewer (1983) and reaching 2020 with Kavanoz (2020), reveals, first of all, lack of ESP TE, secondly research in the field and, thirdly, various suggestions regarding what ESP TE should involve. The suggestions for ESP TE expressed in the literature since 1983 are numerous and too many to refer to in this chapter. A thorough review of the literature in ESP TE can be found in Kakoulli Constantinou (2020). It is important to highlight though, the suggestions for ESP practitioners' involvement in action research for PD (Kavanoz, 2020), Sharpling's (2002) preference towards collaborative interaction in PD and lifelong learning, and Basturkmen's (2014) suggestion for ESP TE focusing on the ESP practitioners' needs in their own educational contexts. ESP TE endeavours should be based on a review of current ESP TE research. The online course that was designed in the context of this study was built on a thorough review of ESP TE literature.

2.5. Designing the curriculum

Through the years, different curriculum development processes appeared in the literature, such as the forward, the central, and the backward design of curriculum development (Richards, 2013). According to the backward design or understanding by design framework (Wiggins & McTighe, 2005), course designers should first decide on the desired results and then specify the content and methods of the curriculum. In other words, the learning outcomes are decided based on the learners' needs, and these determine the curriculum. According to Wiggins and McTighe (2005), a backward design helps learners (or in this case teachers) and course facilitators gain a better understanding of the performance goals, and makes them more aware of whether these goals have been achieved or not, and also how they can be better achieved. ESP TE programmes can be designed following the backward design so that teachers become more aware of the purposes of each course unit, activity, or resource. The ReTEESP Online was designed based on the backward design process as suggested by Wiggins and McTighe (2005, pp. 17-29).

3. Setting the scene

3.1. The purpose of the study

The purpose of the study was the design of an intervention, an online ESP TE course to address the neglected need for ESP TE among a group of 24 language instructors, who wished to educate themselves on issues pertaining to ESP teaching methodology or update their knowledge on the latest developments in ESP teaching practices.

3.2. Methodology

The methodology used was TAR developing in cycles of continuous improvement during the period 2017-2019. This chapter concentrates only on the first steps of the first cycle, which involve the design of the intervention, the ReTEESP Online. The other parts of the study which followed involved the implementation of the course, reflection, course refinement, reimplementation of the refined course, reflection, and drawing of final conclusions; those parts of the study are not described in the present chapter.

3.3. The participants

A total of 24 English language educators from different countries participated in the study. These language instructors were ESP educators representing different ESP fields or English as a Foreign Language (EFL) teachers; their common characteristic was their wish to receive education on issues related to ESP teaching. Table 1 shows the 24 participants in the study for whom ReTEESP Online was designed.

Table 1. The participants in the study

English language instructors		N=24	%
Place of work	Sudan	1	4.16%
	Saudi Arabia	4	16.6%
	Greece	9	37.5%
	Spain	2	8.33%
	United Kingdom	1	4.16%
	Cyprus	5	20.8%
	Egypt	1	4.16%
	Kosovo	1	4.16%
Sex	Male	3	12.5%
	Female	21	87.5%
Age	20-29	3	12.5%
	30-39	8	33.3%
	40-49	8	33.3%
	50-59	3	12.5%
	No response	2	8.33%
Years of experience as an ESP practitioner	0	7	29.16%
	1-5	7	29.16%
	6-10	2	8.33%
	11-15	4	16.66%
	16-20	2	8.33%
	Over 20	2	8.33%
Current position	Higher Education (HE)	16	66.66%
	Vocational Education (VE)	4	16.66%
	Secondary Education (SE)	1	4.16%
	Primary Education (PE)	1	4.16%
	PE, SE, VE	2	8.33%

As Table 1 shows, most of the participants worked in Greece (37.5%, n=9), Cyprus (20.83%, n=5), Saudi Arabia (16.66%, n=4), and Spain (8.33%, n=2), and 66.66% of them (n=16) taught in HE. The majority (75%, n=18) had multiple duties to perform, such as course design, teaching, materials selection, materials development, course evaluation, and research. Teachers' years of experience showed that 14 out of 24 participants were new in the ESP field. This implied that the course that would be designed had to cater for teachers at the beginning stages of ESP teaching.

Concerning the training in ESP teaching which they had received in the past, 58.33% of the participants (n=14) had received some form of ESP training, while 41.66% (n=10) had received no ESP training at all. The participants that had received training in ESP had done so as part of their Bachelor or Master of Arts (BA or MA) studies (n=5, 20.83%), through a combination of BA/MA/PhD studies and seminars, conferences and lectures on ESP (n=5, 20.83%), seminars, conferences, and lectures on ESP solely (n=3, 12.5%), or in-service training (n=1, 4.16%).

4. Method

4.1. Data collection tools

The data for the design of the ReTEESP Online were elicited through:

- a review of the literature on ESP, learning theories, language TE, ESP TE, and recent literature on curriculum development;

- an analysis of the 24 language instructors' needs through (1) an online questionnaire distributed before the course and (2) the participants' comments on the course platform (Google Classroom) at the beginning of the course. The questionnaire created was based on previous research in the field of ESP TE and language TE in general and consisted of 19 items in the form of closed-ended questions (multiple response and Likert scale) and open-ended questions. It was administered to the participants before the beginning of the course via Google Forms; and

- a pilot implementation of the course (Kakoulli Constantinou, Papadima-Sophocleous, & Souleles, 2019) that took place during May 2nd and June 29th, 2017 with six ESP practitioners from HE, who represented a convenience sample (inspired by Cohen, Manion, & Morrison, 2007). During this phase, data were gathered though the online questionnaire discussed above, participants' reflective journals, the facilitator's field notes, comments on Google Classroom, and focus groups.

4.2. Data analysis

Quantitative data elicited from the online questionnaire were analysed using IBM's SPSS 22 software, and descriptive statistics were used to talk about the results. The qualitative data from the questionnaire and participants' comments on the platform were analysed thematically using NVivo 12 software for qualitative data analysis. The review of the literature, the needs analysis, and the pilot study yielded a rich amount of data, which are briefly discussed in the next section.

5. Results and discussion

5.1. The results of the literature review

A brief summary of the literature review on which the ReTEESP Online was based is presented in Section 2 of this chapter. Being guided by the most important findings from the review, the course concentrated on the most important principles of ESP, such as its characteristics, the significance of needs analysis, authenticity, the complex role of the ESP practitioner, and the latest developments in the field, including the integration of new technologies.

Furthermore, following the latest developments in TE, the course adopted a sociocultural approach to TE with elements from the reflective model for TE and critical pedagogy, based on social constructivist and connectivist theories of learning. Moreover, since the participants in the course worked in different geographical locations, the course was designed to be offered online based on the principles of efficient online TE. The course also incorporated suggestions from previous research conducted in the field of ESP TE. These, as well as other aspects of the course, were also determined by needs analysis.

5.2. Needs analysis

The needs analysis process revealed details related to the profiles of the 24 language instructors, reasons for which they decided to attend the course, the knowledge they wished to gain, and information on their Information Technology (IT) literacy. Due to the fact that 41.66% (n=10) of the teachers had received no ESP training and 58.33% (n=14) of them were new to the ESP field, the course had to familiarise them with basic ESP principles before moving to the latest developments in the field. The reasons for which they decided to attend the course are presented in Table 2.

Table 2. Reasons for attending an ESP TE course

Reasons	N	Percent	Percent of Cases
Improvement of teaching methodology	22	22.7%	91.7%
Professional development	21	21.6%	87.5%
Improvement of syllabus design skills	16	16.5%	66.7%
Sharing ideas with other ESP educators	14	14.4%	58.3%
Networking	13	13.4%	54.2%
Self-esteem increase	6	6.2%	25.0%
Employer satisfaction	2	2.1%	8.3%
Promotion	2	2.1%	8.3%
Salary increase	1	1.0%	4.2%
	97	100.0%	404.2%

The fourth column, which presents the percentage of cases, refers to the numbers of ticks each reason got by the participants in the study; in other words, how many times this response was selected by the participants. As Table 2 illustrates, language instructors wished to attend an ESP TE course mainly to improve their teaching methodology, develop professionally, improve their syllabus design skills, and share ideas with colleagues in the field. In their comments on the Google Classroom platform, participants stated that they wished to become members of a network of ESP practitioners that would provide them with the opportunity to exchange ideas on ESP issues (n=8, 33.33%), and upgrade their knowledge on ESP (n=7, 29.16%). Other reasons mentioned were PD (n=1, 4.16%), the facilitator's acquaintance with one of the participants and her appreciation towards the institution she worked for and the training programmes they provided (n=1, 4.16%), and also the fact that the course appeared different and more interesting than other courses (n=1, 4.16%).

Chapter 5

In relation to the knowledge they wished to gain from the course, the teachers stated that they wished to learn about issues of ESP teaching methodology including the integration of new technologies (n=8, 33.33%), the latest developments in ESP (n=5, 20.83%), and how to improve as ESP professionals (n=3, 12.5%). They also mentioned ESP course planning and syllabus design (n=3, 12.5%), assessment methods (n=1, 4.16%), new ESP material (n=1, 4.16%), and resources for continuous PD (n=1, 4.16%). Four participants (16%) also repeated that they wished to participate in a professional network dealing with ESP issues, where they could learn from each other's experiences. These findings are very similar to the findings of Bocanegra-Valle and Basturkmen (2019), which proves that the needs of ESP practitioners are similar in different areas of the world.

Finally, the data revealed information on the teachers' IT literacy, which was important, as the course would be offered online, since the participants resided in different countries. It was decided that the ReTEESP Online would be offered using the G Suite for Education, YouTube, email, Skype, and Facebook. The G Suite for Education was considered to be appropriate for the delivery of the course, since as a cloud-based technology it was cost effective, convenient, practical, flexible, with high scalability (González-Martínez, Bote-Lorenzo, Gómez-Sánchez, & Cano-Parra, 2015). For this reason, it was essential to ask the participants how familiar they were with technology and these tools in particular. The results are illustrated in Figure 1 and Figure 2.

Figure 1. Participants' competency in using technologies in their teaching

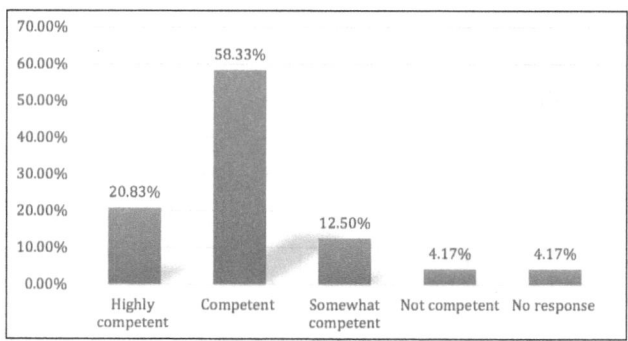

Figure 2. Participants' familiarity with technologies used in the ReTEESP Online

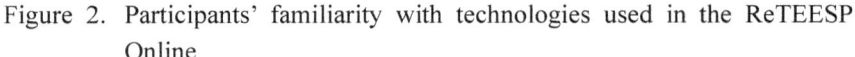

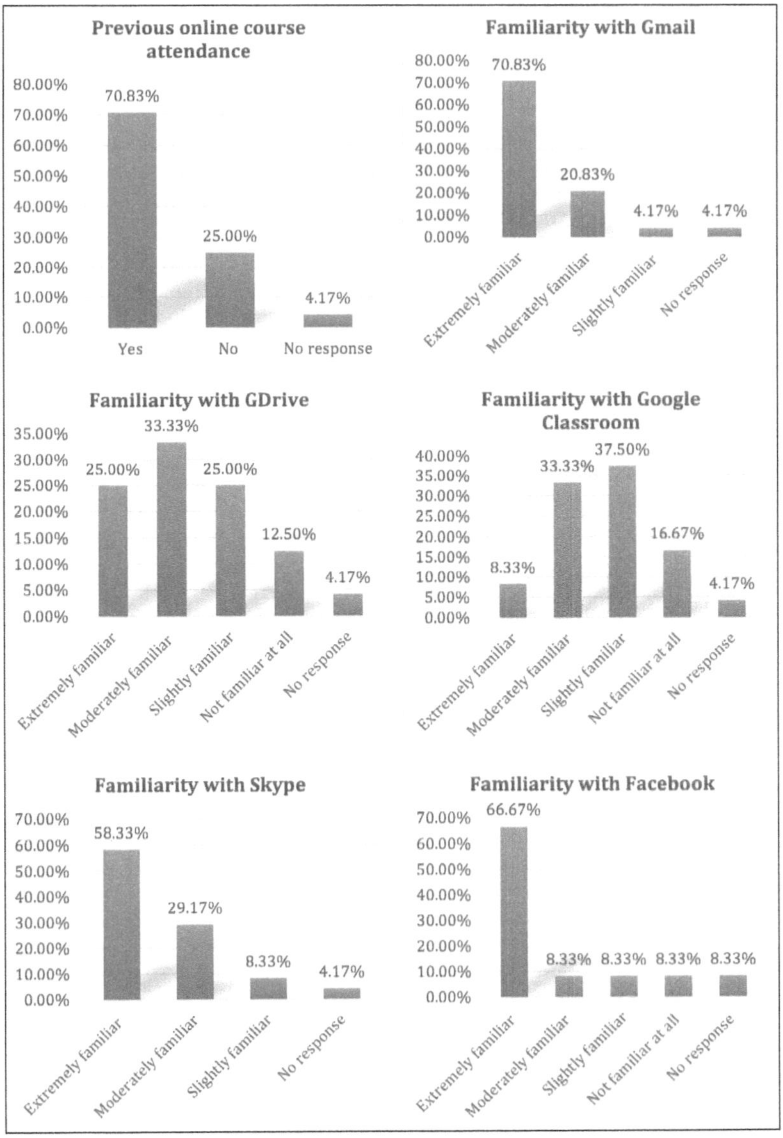

As illustrated in Figure 2, 25% of the participants (n=6) had no experience of attending an online course. Furthermore, even though 17 of them (70.83%) were extremely familiar with the use of Gmail, some participants had not been acquainted with Google Drive or Google Classroom in the past. Regarding Skype and Facebook, the majority of the participants were extremely and moderately familiar with the tools, possibly because they used them in their personal lives. These results indicated that the participants would need guidance regarding the use of the G Suite for Education tools, such as Google Classroom and the Google Drive, through the course, which meant that the facilitator should be in constant communication with the teachers, and that clear guidelines should be uploaded on the course platform.

5.3. ReTEESP Online pilot implementation

The findings from the trial implementation of the ReTEESP Online generated important implications for the design of the course and its actual implementation. With regard to the qualitative data that were received from ESP practitioners' reflective journals, their comments on Google Classroom, facilitator's field notes, and the focus groups conducted at the end of the programme, thematic analysis yielded three general thematic categories: (1) participants' professional experiences, (2) the course experience, and (3) suggestions for improvement of the course. The analysis revealed many positive aspects of the course, such as the knowledge acquired, the participants' high performance in the course, teachers' positive perceptions on the technologies used, etc. It also revealed different challenges faced during the course, such as teachers' failure to meet the deadlines, difficulties in collaboration in some cases, technical difficulties, etc. and suggestions for improvement, such as the course duration, the organisation of content, presentation of material, etc.

The findings from the pilot phase yielded useful results for the design and the actual implementation of the course. These findings are explained in detail in Kakoulli Constantinou et al.'s (2019) chapter in the edited volume *ESP teaching and teacher education: current theories and practices*.

5.4. ReTEESP Online: the curriculum design

Based on all the above, the ReTEESP Online was designed to be a flexible, online ESP TE course of three to six weeks, five hours per week, intended for ESP educators representing different ESP fields or EFL educators who would like to educate themselves on issues pertaining to ESP teaching methodology or update their knowledge on the latest developments in ESP teaching practices. The aim of the course was to engage educators in hands-on activities that would enable them to develop in areas associated with ESP teaching and give them the opportunity to implement their new knowledge in their ESP practice. A general overview of the course can be found in a brief weekly outline provided in supplementary materials, Appendix A. Additionally, a detailed description of the last session of course (Session 6 – Sharing thoughts and reflecting collaboratively) provided in supplementary materials, Appendix B, serves as an example of how the learning theories and the TE models the course was founded on were realised in the course. More specifically, the description of Session 6 shows the types of activities and the technology tools that were employed in the course, as well as the role of the facilitator and the active role of the participants in the course. The description of Session 6 was based on the backward design template, as suggested by Wiggins and McTighe (2005, p. 22).

The course was first of all based on the literature review, as this is discussed in Section 2 of this chapter. It was therefore led by social constructivism (Vygotsky, 1978) and connectivism (Siemens, 2005), adopting a sociocultural approach to TE (Belcher, 2004) with elements from the reflective model for PD (Wallace, 1991) and critical pedagogy (Hawkins & Norton, 2009), and it was also based on previous research conducted in the area of ESP TE. These theories and TE models were realised through interactive and collaborative activities, such as discussions on Google Classroom using the 'Comment' feature underneath posts, collaboration on Google docs for the design of ESP tasks and lesson plans, sharing of ideas, provision of feedback to peers, and through the compilation of reflective journals (see Session 6 in supplementary materials, Appendix B). The course was also based on a 'practising what you preach' approach (Wallace,

1991), since the techniques and methods of instruction which were used in the course could be used by teachers in their language classrooms. ReTEESP Online also incorporated principles of critical pedagogy, since it embraced and respected the teachers' different educational contexts providing teachers with the opportunity to talk about their own educational realities and find solutions to their own problems. Generally, the course was designed to be delivered through interactive online lectures, online discussions, independent reading, writing, listening, independent research, and individual and collaborative online work. The tools used for the delivery of the course were the G Suite for Education, YouTube, email, Skype, and Facebook, as these technologies had all the affordances needed to serve the learning theories and TE models the course was built on (Kakoulli Constantinou, 2018, 2019). In order to ensure that the course would be implemented successfully, the principles of online TE (Henry & Meadows, 2008; Maggioli, 2012; Powell & Bodur, 2019), as discussed in Section 2.3, were followed throughout the course.

Furthermore, the topics (as outlined in supplementary materials, Appendix A) were based on a review of research in ESP (Section 2.1), and also aimed at satisfying teachers' needs, as these were identified by needs analysis (Section 5.2). The literature review on ESP revealed that the core aspects of ESP are (1) needs analysis (Belcher, 2009; Dudley-Evans & St John, 1998; Flowerdew, 2013; Johns & Makalela, 2011), (2) authenticity of material and tasks (Benavent & Penamaria, 2011), and (3) the multifaceted role of the ESP practitioner (Dudley-Evans & St John, 1998; Johns, 2013). For this reason, these aspects were incorporated in the themes that ReTEESP Online covered. As far as needs analysis is concerned, since many of the teachers had limited experience in teaching ESP, it was decided that they needed to be introduced to ESP and its nature and the basic concepts of ESP had to be stressed in the course. Moreover, the ESP lesson plan was regarded as a useful way of approaching all aspects of the ESP lesson, from designing the lesson to setting the learning outcomes, deciding on material and tasks. Moreover, the needs analysis revealed that the teachers had to be provided with guidance on the use of technology. For this reason, the first session was dedicated to an introduction to the course and the technologies used for its delivery, and constant guidance was provided to teachers through email, private messages on Messenger, and guidelines posted on Google Classroom. Being in line with the teachers' wishes, the course also provided the teachers with knowledge on how they could continue developing professionally, even after the completion of the course, familiarising them with professional ESP associations and events, and also creating the appropriate conditions for sustaining the network of professionals that had been created (e.g. through keeping the Facebook private group created by the facilitator active). This was also in accordance with the connectivist approach governing the course.

Finally, the course pilot implementation helped in its fine tuning. More specifically, the course duration was made more flexible (ranging from three to six weeks), and the positive aspects of the course were strengthened, while the weaknesses were addressed taking into consideration the participants' suggestions.

6. Conclusions

This chapter presented the design of an online ESP TE course, based on a review of the literature; an analysis of teachers' needs and a pilot implementation of the course. As far as the literature review is concerned, the course was founded on the core principles of ESP, on social constructivism and connectivism, and TE models, such as the reflective model for TE, a sociocultural perspective to TE, and critical language TE. Moreover, the course was built on the principles of successful online TE, it was inspired by previous research conducted in the area of ESP TE, and the curriculum was based on the backward design model for curriculum development. Regarding needs analysis, this also played an important role in the design of ReTEESP Online, since it revealed the aspects on which the course should focus in order to satisfy the needs of the ESP practitioners. Lastly, the pilot implementation of the course, exposed the weaknesses and the strengths of the course, and it helped in its improvement, before its actual implementation.

Due to the limited research in ESP TE and the limited opportunities for ESP TE, this chapter could prove useful to ESP TE researchers, ESP practitioners, ESP

TE educators, course designers, and stakeholders. The value of this research lies in the way the particular intervention, the ESP TE course, was designed and delivered. Even though generalisations may not be possible, the fact that the participants of the study were language instructors from different countries of the world and different educational environments may allow the way the course was designed to be replicated in similar contexts, providing language instructors with the opportunity to receive education in ESP teaching.

7. Acknowledgements

We would like to thank all the language teachers who participated in the first implementation of the ReTEESP Online, as well as the teachers who participated in the pilot study, whose feedback was invaluable.

8. Supplementary materials

https://research-publishing.box.com/s/ofhhyaf64jxocoiap8xim44bzq8ev1cj

References

Abedeen, F. (2015). *Exploration of ESP teacher knowledge and practices at tertiary and applied colleges in Kuwait: implications for pre- and in-service ESP teacher training.* Exeter. https://ore.exeter.ac.uk/repository/bitstream/handle/10871/17437/AbedeenF.pdf?sequence=1

Alousque, I. N. (2016). Developments in ESP: from register analysis to a genre-based and CLIL-based approach. *Revista de Lenguas Para Fines Específicos, 22*(1), 190-212. https://doi.org/10.20420/rlfe.2016.310

Álvarez-Mayo, C., Gallagher-Brett, A., & Michel, F. (2017). (Eds). *Innovative language teaching and learning at university: enhancing employability.* Research-publishing.net. https://doi.org/10.14705/rpnet.2017.innoconf2016.9781908416506

Basturkmen, H. (2010). *Developing courses in English for specific purposes.* Palgrave Macmillan.

Basturkmen, H. (2014). LSP teacher education: review of literature and suggestions for the research agenda. *Ibérica: Revista de La Asociación Europea de Lenguas Para Fines Específicos (AELFE), 28*(Fall), 17-34.

Belcher, D. D. (2004). Trends in teaching English for specific purposes. *Annual Review of Applied Linguisitics, 24*(2004), 165-186.

Belcher, D. D. (2009). What ESP is and can be: an introduction. In D. D. Belcher (Ed.), *English for specific purposes in theory and practice* (pp. 1-20). The University of Michigan Press.

Benavent, G. T., & Penamaria, S. S.-R. (2011). Use of authentic materials in the ESP classroom. *Encuentro, 20*, 89-94. http://search.proquest.com/docview/968114142?accountid=14391

Bezukladnikov, K., & Kruze, B. (2012). An outline of an ESP teacher training course. *World Applied Sciences Journal, 20*(Special Issue of Pedagogy and Psychology), 103-106.

Bocanegra-Valle, A., & Basturkmen, H. (2019). Investigating the teacher education needs of experienced ESP teachers in Spanish universities. *Iberica, 38*, 127-150.

Bracaj, M. (2014). Teaching English for specific purposes and teacher training. *European Scientific Journal, 10*(2), 40-49.

Chen, Y. (2012). ESP development in Taiwan: an overview. *ESP News, TESOL International Association,* (August). http://newsmanager.commpartners.com/tesolespis/issues/2012-08-21/2.html

Cohen, L., Manion, L., & Morrison, K. (2007). *Research methods in education* (6th ed.). Routledge. https://doi.org/10.1111/j.1467-8527.2007.00388_4.x

Dede, C. (2006). Introduction. In C. Dede (Ed.), *Online professional development for teachers: emerging models and methods* (pp. 1-11). Harvard Education Press.

Dudley-Evans, T., & St John, M. J. (1998). *Developments in English for specific purposes: a multi-disciplinary approach.* Cambridge University Press.

Ewer, J. R. (1983). Teacher training for EST: problems and methods. *The ESP Journal, 2*(1), 9-31.

Flowerdew, L. (2013). Needs analysis and curriculum development in ESP. In B. Paltridge & S. Starfield (Eds), *The handbook of English for specific purposes* (pp. 325-346). John Wiley & Sons, Inc. https://doi.org/10.1002/9781118339855.ch17

González-Martínez, J. A., Bote-Lorenzo, M. L., Gómez-Sánchez, E., & Cano-Parra, R. (2015). Cloud computing and education: a state-of-the-art survey. *Computers and Education, 80*, 132-151. https://doi.org/10.1016/j.compedu.2014.08.017

Hawkins, M., & Norton, B. (2009). Critical language teacher education. In A. Burns & J. C. Richards (Eds), *The Cambridge guide to second language teacher education* (pp. 30-39). Cambridge University Press.

Henry, J., & Meadows, J. (2008). An absolutely riveting online course: nine principles for excellence in web-based teaching. *Canadian Journal of Learning and Technology, 34*(1). https://doi.org/10.21432/t20c7f

Hutchinson, T., & Waters, A. (1987). *English for English for specific purposes: a learning-centered approach.* Cambridge University Press.

Johns, A. M. (2013). The history of English for specific purposes research. In B. Paltridge & S. Starfield (Eds), *The handbook of English for specific purposes* (pp. 5-30). Wiley Blackwell. https://doi.org/10.1002/9781118339855.ch1

Johns, A. M., & Makalela, L. (2011). Needs analysis, critical ethnography, and context: perspectives from the client - and the consultant. In D. D. Belcher, A. M. Johns, & B. Paltridge (Eds), *New directions in English for specific purposes research* (pp. 197-221). The University of Michigan Press. https://doi.org/10.3998/mpub.371075

Kakoulli Constantinou, E. (2018). Teaching in clouds: using the G Suite for Education for the delivery of two English for academic purposes courses. *The Journal of Teaching English for Specific and Academic Purposes, 6*(2), 305-317. https://doi.org/10.22190/jtesap1802305c

Kakoulli Constantinou, E. (2019). Revisiting the cloud: reintegrating the G Suite for Education in English for specific purposes teaching. In C. N. Giannikas, E. Kakoulli Constantinou, & S. Papadima-Sophocleous (Eds), *Professional development in CALL: a selection of papers* (pp. 55-69). Research-publishing.net. https://doi.org/10.14705/rpnet.2019.28.870

Kakoulli Constantinou, E. (2020). *English for specific purposes teacher education: a technical action research study.* Unpublished doctoral dissertation. Cyprus University of Technology, Cyprus.

Kakoulli Constantinou, E., Papadima-Sophocleous, S., & Souleles, N. (2019). Finding the way through the ESP maze: designing an ESP teacher education programme. In S. Papadima-Sophocleous, E. Kakoulli Constantinou, & C. N. Giannikas (Eds), *ESP teaching and teacher education: current theories and practices* (pp. 27-46). Research-publishing.net. https://doi.org/10.14705/rpnet.2019.33.924

Kavanoz, S. (2020). Use of action research as a viable paradigm for the professional development of ESP instructors. In N. Kenny, E. E. Işık-Taş & H. Jian (Eds), *English for specific purposes instruction and research: current practices, challenges and innovations* (pp. 247-265). https://doi.org/10.1007/978-3-030-32914-3_13

Maggioli, G. D. (2012). *Teaching language teachers: scaffolding professional learning.* Rowman & Littlefield Education.

Mahapatra, S. K. (2011). Teacher training in ESP: a historical review. *English for Specific Purposes World, 11*(33), 1-15. http://esp-world.info/Articles_33/Doc/Teacher%20Training%20in%20ESP%20A%20Historical%20Review_Mahapatra.pdf

Powell, C. G., & Bodur, Y. (2019). Teachers' perceptions of an online professional development experience: implications for a design and implementation framework. *Teaching and Teacher Education, 77*, 19-30. https://doi.org/10.1016/j.tate.2018.09.004

Richards, J. C. (2001). *Curriculum development in language teaching.* Cambridge University Press.

Richards, J. C. (2013). Curriculum approaches in language teaching: forward, central, and backward design. *RELC Journal, 44*(1), 5-33. https://doi.org/10.1177/0033688212473293

Richards, J. C., & Farrell, T. S. C. (2005). *Professional development for language teachers: strategies for teacher learning.* Cambridge University Press.

Richardson, V. (1997). Constructivist teaching and teacher education: theory and practice. In V. Richardson (Ed.), *Constructivist teacher education: building a world of new understandings.* (pp. 3-14). Falmer Press. https://doi.org/10.4324/9780203973684

Selevičienė, E. (2020). *Effectiveness and acceptance of Web 2.0 technologies in the studies of English for specific purposes in higher education.* Doctoral dissertation. Mykolas Romeris University, Lithuania. https://repository.mruni.eu/handle/007/16489

Sharpling, G. (2002). Learning to teach English for academic purposes: some current training and development issues. *English Language Teacher Education and Development, 6*, 82-94.

Siemens, G. (2005). Connectivism: a learning theory for the digital age. *International Journal of Instructional Technology and Distance Learning, 1*, 1-8.

Vygotsky, L. S. (1978). *Mind in society: the development of higher mental processes.* Harvard University Press.

Wallace, M. J. (1991). *Training foreign language teachers. A reflective approach.* Cambridge University Press.

Wenger, E. C. (1998). *Communities of practice: learning, meaning and identity.* Cambridge University Press.

Wiggins, G., & McTighe, J. (2005). *Understanding by design* (2nd ed.). Association for Supervision and Curriculum Development.

6. Technological mediation in a global competence virtual exchange project: a critical digital literacies perspective

Anna Nicolaou[1]

Abstract

The changing cultural and social landscape of our world today, along with the emergence of various technologies, has redefined 21st century societies. In light of these changes, new pedagogical approaches have been implemented to support civic life, education, and communication in our highly complex, digitised era (Pegrum, Dudeney, & Hockly, 2018). One such approach is virtual exchange, a technologically-mediated practice which involves engaging classes in online intercultural interaction and collaboration projects with geographically dispersed partners (O'Dowd, 2007, 2019). Many studies (Helm, 2014; Hauck & Satar, 2018; Vinagre, 2016) have examined the role of technology in virtual exchange projects as well as the development of various digital competences, along with linguistic and intercultural learning. The present study contributes to the discussion pertaining to the role of technology in the virtual exchange context adding a critical digital literacies perspective manifested in the use of technology for global competence development and as a social praxis (Ávila & Pandya, 2013). Specifically, the study aims at exploring the students' perceptions about digital skills development through their participation in a global competence virtual exchange project, as well as the ways in which students interact with technology in order to develop global competence and active citizenship.

---

1. Cyprus University of Technology, Limassol, Cyprus; anna.nicolaou@cut.ac.cy; https://orcid.org/0000-0001-8052-2201

How to cite: Nicolaou, A. (2021). Technological mediation in a global competence virtual exchange project: a critical digital literacies perspective. In S. Papadima-Sophocleous, E. Kakoulli Constantinou & C. N. Giannikas (Eds), *Tertiary education language learning: a collection of research* (pp. 111-131). Research-publishing.net. https://doi.org/10.14705/rpnet.2021.51.1257

Chapter 6

Keywords: virtual exchange, critical digital literacies, global competence, active citizenship.

1. Introduction

In a globalised world characterised by increased mobility and expanded access to technology, the need for new, 21st century skills has emerged (Dudeney & Hockly, 2016). The vast social and technological changes, along with a greater movement of people, knowledge, and ideas across borders (BrckaLorenz & Gieser, 2011), has created a world that is ever more interconnected and interdependent (Mansilla, Jackson, & Jacobs, 2013). With this reality in mind, many educational institutions have recognised the pressing need for including global perspectives in their education (Cushner & Brennan, 2007) while at the same appreciating the emerging nature of digital literacies which can support educational, professional, personal, social, and civic lives (Pegrum et al., 2018). In light of these efforts, new teaching methodologies embracing Web 2.0 technologies have been utilised in order to support innovative pedagogical interventions aiming at addressing intercultural, global, and digital objectives. One pedagogical approach that can foster global competence and the ability to "effectively navigate an increasingly digital world" (Dudeney & Hockly, 2016, p. 115) is virtual exchange. This study aims at exploring university students' perceptions about digital skills development through their participation in a global competence virtual exchange project as well as at examining the ways in which students interact with technology in order to develop global competence and active citizenship.

1.1. Literature review

Virtual exchange, or telecollaboration, is a technologically sustained practice which involves engaging classes in online intercultural interaction and collaboration projects with geographically dispersed partners (O'Dowd, 2007, 2019). Telecollaboration projects can combine synchronous or asynchronous interaction through a variety of Web 2.0 tools, such as threaded discussion boards, wikis, blogs, social networking sites, videoconferencing software, virtual learning environments, or 3D virtual worlds. The way virtual exchange tasks and interactions are carried out has evolved over time as more sophisticated tools and applications have become increasingly available for use (Godwin-Jones, 2019). Earlier asynchronous email and text-based collaborations which offered participants adequate time to reflect on their interactions (Helm, 2015) were followed by more recent configurations. These relied on synchronous communication, as a result of the emergence of platforms which afford audio and video interactions between participants which are more direct and efficient due to ubiquitous mobile connection (Godwin-Jones, 2019).

Previous studies (Hauck & Kurek, 2017; Hauck & Satar, 2018; Helm, 2014; Kurek & Turula, 2014; O'Rourke & Stickler, 2017; Vinagre, 2016) have examined the role of technology in telecollaborative projects as well as the development of various digital competences, along with linguistic and intercultural learning, as a major outcome of participation in intercultural encounters. For example, Helm (2014) examined the development of digital literacies through virtual exchange in foreign language education. Specifically, Helm explored the types of computer literacies virtual exchange projects fostered by analysing bilingual and lingua franca exchange projects between the University of Padova and other universities in Europe. In these exchanges, students used synchronous and asynchronous communication tools through which they developed competences such as computer-mediated collaboration, content creation, sharing, decision-making, negotiation, and privacy.

Recently, new virtual exchange configurations have emerged, following the changes in our current world which is characterised by increased global communication, mobility, and digital connectivity. The development of "active, informed, and responsible citizens who are tolerant of difference and who are actively engaged in political and democratic processes" (O'Dowd, 2018, p. 21) seems to be a critical need in an interconnected and interdependent world. With this in mind, virtual exchange can be envisioned to provide a sufficient initiative for enabling learners to cross global boundaries and come to terms with the demands of the 21st century as universal citizens who are empowered to respond to diverse global and local problems of our contemporary society through their transnational partnerships (Nicolaou & Sevilla-Pavón, 2016).

This important evolution of virtual exchange has prompted the exploration of technological mediation in a critical and global citizenship perspective (Godwin-Jones, 2019; O'Dowd, 2019). A case in point is Helm's (2013) study, which outlined the development of multimodal communication through the *Soliya Connect Program*. This remarkable project facilitated intercultural dialogue between students in the United States, Europe, and the Middle East. In these exchanges, students engaged in synchronous multimodal audio, video, and text conversations around issues pertaining to conflicting topics such as terrorism, religion, and violence. The *Soliya Connect Program* offers a different telecollaboration approach that can educate globally competent students and citizens (Elliott-Gower & Hill, 2015) and is an example of how technology can be utilised with a view to cultivating democratic values and fostering global citizenship in a 'superdiverse era' (Pegrum et al., 2018). A more recent report by Hauck (2019) discussed the concept of *critical digital literacy* and how this can be developed through virtual exchange initiatives. Hauck (2019) explained that critical digital literacy entails the ability to exercise agency, which is mediated by contextual factors, such as sites, tools, and applications utilised by participants in order to interact with their distant partners. In this sense, technology is viewed as a significant contextual element which participants interact with and this interaction results in the emergence of multiple affordances for competence learning and the enactment of individual or collective agency. Hauck (2019) examined digital-pedagogical competence development of future teachers. To assess the development of competences the study was informed by the Technological Pedagogical Content Knowledge (TPACK) framework (Mishra & Koehler, 2006). The particular study highlighted the positive impact of virtual exchange on both the awareness of the role of technology and the attitude towards the use of technological tools in educational interventions. It also drew attention to the use of technology both as a mediating element and a learning outcome of virtual exchange initiatives. In addition, the study underlined the development of multiple competences such as linguistic competence, flexibility, and interaction which intersect with digital competences. Finally, the study emphasised the concept of criticality in terms of critical awareness of the pedagogical affordances of the tools used in the exchange, and points to the lack of the critical perspective of digital literacy that guides participants of virtual exchange projects beyond the functional uses of technology by critically engaging them in the socio-political context of the exchange (Hauck, 2019). Similarly, a recent study by Kopish and Marques (2020) explored the extent to which a transnational, collaborative curricular project based on the Collaborative Online International Learning (COIL) approach contributed to pre-service teachers' development of global and emerging digital competences. In this study, Kopish and Marques (2020) confirmed the potential of virtual exchange for the development of the aforementioned competences; however, they noted the absence of evidenced enhancement of global competence in the form of taking action in the world.

1.2. Theoretical background

The present study contributes to the discussion pertaining to the role of technology in the virtual exchange context adding a critical digital literacies perspective to the technological mediation that sustains telecollaboration projects. As virtual exchange projects are inherently technologically-mediated, the role of technology and how learners interact with the wide array of technological tools used in projects is considered to be crucial. Equally significant is how participants reflect upon the mediating role of online communication in their interactions (O'Dowd, 2016). This process of reflection is particularly significant in global competence virtual exchange projects that aspire to build the learners' internationalised profile and promote democratic participation and active involvement in society by empowering the participants to take action for improving the lives of people in the community. Mansilla et al. (2013) delineated the characteristics of globally competent students, which include the ability to delve into the world's most significant problems by conducting appropriate research, to recognise and respect others' and their own perspectives, to communicate ideas with audiences of diverse backgrounds successfully, and to be empowered to take action and participate reflectively in order to improve conditions. Byram (2008) referred to intercultural citizenship for foreign language education as part of a broader citizenship education which transcends national boundaries and places emphasis on teaching and learning which leads to action in the world. Intercultural citizenship entails awareness and respect of self and others, willingness to interact with culturally diverse groups, as well as the acquisition of knowledge and skills that enables learners to actively participate in today's complex social contexts (Jackson, 2011).

The concepts of critical activism and democratic participation are also emphasised in van Lier's (2004) ecological theory. Informed by van Lier's notions of criticality and agency, this study explores the technological mediation in a virtual exchange project which aimed at developing university students' global competence and active citizenship. In learning, agency is a concept related to autonomy, intrinsic motivation, investment, volition, and intentionality, initiated by social, interactional, cultural, institutional, and other contextual factors (van Lier, 2004, 2008). Van Lier (2010) explains that agency can emerge individually or collectively when learners need to make choices and when they are provided with opportunities to work as participants in a community of learners. Creating a learning context that affords the emergence and development of agency is crucial in pedagogical design (van Lier, 2008).

The notion of criticality can be linked with an action-oriented approach in language education, which provides a dynamic and holistic vision necessary in our ever-changing societies (Piccardo & North, 2019). Van Lier (2004) emphasises the "democratic goal in our educational endeavours" (p. 79) and explains that the task of democracy that education serves is oriented towards critical activism. The present study also draws from the concept of critical digital literacy manifested in the use of technology as social praxis (Ávila & Pandya, 2013). According to Pangrazio (2016), critical digital literacy is based upon a transcendental perspective which links digital activity to the concepts of freedom, democracy and civic engagement. In this sense, the acquisition of technical skills is used to accomplish positive changes both for the individual and the broader social context. With this in mind, this study examines the technological mediation in virtual exchange projects guided by the following research questions.

- What are the students' perceptions about digital skills development through their participation in a global competence virtual exchange project?

- How do students interact with technology in order to develop global competence and active citizenship?

2. Method

This study adopted Design-Based Research (DBR) as its underlying methodology. As mentioned in Nicolaou and Sevilla-Pavón (2017, p. 591), DBR (Brown, 1992; Collins, 1992) is an emerging paradigm for the study of learning in context through the systematic design and study of instructional strategies and tools in iterative cycles of enactment, reflection, refinement, and redesign (Collins, 1992). DBR is deemed to be a useful paradigm in technologically-mediated projects, such as virtual exchange, where the learning process expands from a traditional classroom and where technological developments support learning and learning processes (Ørngreen, 2015). According to Juuti and Lavonen (2006), DBR involves a designer, (researcher), a practitioner (teacher), and an artefact (web-based learning environment). In the case of virtual exchange projects, the web-based environment plays a crucial role in successful or failed interaction and collaboration between the learners. As O'Dowd (2019) proposes, emerging frameworks of virtual exchange should offer opportunities for "increasing awareness to how intercultural communication is mediated by online technologies and how social media can shape the creation and interpretation of messages" (p. 23). Within the framework of a DBR design which included an exploration, an implementation and a reflection phase, this paper reports on the third iterative cycle of the implementation of a virtual exchange project.

2.1. Settings

The study is situated within the Youth Entrepreneurship for Society (YES) virtual exchange project carried out between a Cypriot and a Spanish university. The

Chapter 6

YES project was a social entrepreneurship virtual exchange project designed with a critical approach, and was an attempt to expand telecollaborative content-based language learning by connecting dispersed, culturally diverse students at two universities as well as by involving local Non-Government Organisations (NGOs) based in the two participating countries, Cyprus and Spain (Nicolaou & Sevilla-Pavón, 2018; Sevilla-Pavón & Nicolaou, 2020). The project was a pedagogical intervention which was implemented with an ecological perspective on learning, thus viewing technology as an important mediating contextual element, offering opportunities for meaningful interaction, critical co-creation of knowledge, and exercising of social agency within a real-life context. The project aimed to link the classroom with the local community and to foster students' global competences (Council of Europe, 2016) and active citizenship, as well as to promote youth participation in society through digital innovation. The YES project was embedded in two English for Specific Purposes (ESP) modules at two higher education institutions. Specifically, the YES project connected 39 students of Business Management at a Cypriot university and 19 students of International Business at a Spanish university. The intervention involved the use of English as a lingua franca and communication modes included synchronous and asynchronous interaction in a blended learning environment. Web 2.0 tools included the use of Google applications as well as additional learning management systems and multimedia software (Nicolaou & Sevilla-Pavón, 2018; Sevilla-Pavón & Nicolaou, 2020). Table 1 summarises the technologies used in the virtual exchange in connection to the project's tasks and activities. For more details about the task sequence of this project see Sevilla-Pavón and Nicolaou (2019).

Table 1. Technologies, tasks and activities

Technologies	Tasks and activities
Google+	Creation of individual digital profiles
Google+ Communities	Asynchronous communication in the form of posts, comments, sharing of text, images, and multimedia files, such as digital stories
Google Mail	Asynchronous communication among students, between students and teachers, and between students and NGO representatives

Google docs	Collaborative creation of documents, such as problem-solving reports, and digital stories scripts
Google slides	Collaborative creation of presentations and elevator pitches
Movie Maker, iMovie, Animoto, GoAnimate, Photoshop	Collaborative creation of multimedia artefacts, such as digital stories demonstrating innovative, entrepreneurial solutions addressed to current, social problems indicated by local NGOs and volunteer groups

2.2. Participants

This paper reports on the Cypriot perspective of the virtual exchange, focusing on data collected from 39 ESP students of Business Management at the Cyprus University of Technology (CUT). The CUT is a Greek-speaking university that admits students from Cyprus and Greece. The context is rather monocultural and monolingual, and interaction with, and knowledge of, other cultures are minimal or even negligible within the university. Cyprus also ranks quite low in Erasmus youth mobility programmes, both inbound and outbound. It is assumed that the students' limited interaction with peers of diverse backgrounds may play a vital role in shaping their attitudes and openness towards difference and it may affect the development of global competences. At the same time, the university is a *high-tech environment* (Pegrum et al., 2018) and offers to its students the opportunity to work with various technologies.

2.3. Data collection strategies

Qualitative data were collected by means of focus groups and written reflections. Focus groups were conducted upon completion of the project while reflection papers were composed at three stages during the exchange. Transcriptions of focus groups with 30 students, and 98 reflection papers composed by 39 students at the Cypriot university were entered and analysed in the NVivo qualitative research software. The method of Thematic Analysis (TA) was used; "TA is a is a method for identifying analyzing, and interpreting patterns of meaning ('themes') across qualitative data" (Clarke & Braun, 2017, p. 297). To measure the inter-coder reliability, the data set was given to another independent researcher who coded 10%. Cohen's (1960) Kappa was calculated to be 0.69 which, according to Stemler (2001), is considered to be satisfactory.

2.4. Data analysis

In order to answer the research questions, the *revised framework of digital literacies* by Pegrum et al. (2018) was utilised. The framework was first published by Dudeney, Hockly, and Pegrum (2013) and was extended and republished five years later in light of constant technological and cultural, socio-political developments which mandate a more critical perspective on technologies and the information and communication channels they afford (Pegrum et al., 2018). The revised framework comprises four major focus areas: communication, information, collaboration, and (re)design. The focus areas include different literacies, such as multimedia literacy, information literacy, and intercultural literacy. In order to answer the first research question, emphasis was placed in the participants' perceptions of the development of digital literacies. In order to answer the second research question, there was an effort to identify instances whereby direct or indirect connections were made between technological mediation and the development of global competences and active citizenship, during the timeframe of the virtual exchange tasks and activities.

3. Results and discussion

The analysis of data provided insights pertaining to the role of technology in the specific pedagogical intervention, indicating that technological mediation was considered as an important element of the virtual exchange context. The qualitative analysis suggested that the affordances of the technological tools used in the exchange were satisfactorily perceived and utilised by the participants. The students seem to have acquired various digital skills and the sustained interaction with technology appears to have facilitated the development of global competence and active citizenship. In addition, the results of this study add to the discussion around the digital literacy divide which challenges Prensky's (2001) dichotomy of 'digital natives' and 'digital immigrants'. To illustrate, a comment mentioned by Student 29 follows:

> "It was generally nice to learn some things on the Internet: we learned how to use the Drive, Google, the Internet, email. Previously we only used the Internet for Facebook, we did not use any other applications; it was really nice".

In this study, the findings suggest that even though there seems to be some comfort with technology in the 'Net generation' (Tapscott, 1999) and particularly with its social use, this level of comfort does not seem to transfer to learning (Dudeney, 2011). However, the fact that participants were 'tech comfy' facilitated a smooth transformation of technology use from social to more pedagogical (Dudeney, 2011), and contributed to the acquisition of new technological skills and the familiarisation with new tools, such as Google applications.

3.1. Digital skills development

With regard to the first research question, the participants seem to have developed various digital literacies through their participation in the virtual exchange project. One of the competences was multimodal literacy, which was mainly attributed to the Digital Storytelling (DST) task that was included in the project. DST can be defined as the blend of the longstanding art of telling stories and the 21st century practice of putting together a variety of available contemporary multimedia tools, including graphics, audio, video, animation, and web publishing (Lambert, 2013; Robin, 2009). DST is a technologically challenging task which makes it an activity that fosters digital and technology skills (Darvin & Norton, 2014). In this study, participants mentioned their acquired ability to create a short video (digital story) utilising different multimedia tools. An additional literacy that seems to have been developed was search literacy as the participants needed to make effective use of different search engines in order to facilitate communication with their foreign partners and to complete the tasks. Furthermore, security literacy appears to have been enhanced as part of a broader personal literacy. Participants mentioned their acquired knowledge in protecting their digital identity and their privacy in terms of document and image sharing.

Moreover, participants referred to their ability in participating in the online network created for the purposes of the virtual exchange project and building collaborations in order to achieve common goals, indicating the development of network and participatory literacy. Since virtual exchange projects are inherently intercultural, usually aiming at building participants' intercultural communicative competence (Byram, 1997), this project was not an exception. Through the deployment of the recommended synchronous and asynchronous tools (Google applications), as well as through the use of additional preferred communication channels, such as Skype or Facebook, participants developed intercultural literacy in the form of being able to communicate effectively with their foreign counterparts and acquiring knowledge about their culture.

Finally, the development of critical literacy, which is described in the revised framework as the creation of "productive, critical contributions to the world" (Common Sense Education, 2017, cited in Pegrum et al., 2018, p. 10), was manifested in the participants' meaningful engagement with technology in their effort to discuss, research, create, and share innovative digital solutions addressed to local organisations' real social problems (Nicolaou & Sevilla-Pavón, 2018; Sevilla-Pavón & Nicolaou, 2020). Overall, participants in the virtual exchange seem to have developed various digital literacies through their active participation in the project's tasks and activities. Table 2 summarises the participants' development of digital literacies evidenced by verbatim comments.

Table 2. Development of digital literacies

Digital literacies development	Students' quotes
Multimodal literacy	"We were able to make the video (digital story) about our product, using the multimedia that we needed" (Student 26).
Search literacy	"Sometimes it helped us correct ourselves using Google translate and search for information on the Internet in different websites" (Student 28).

Security literacy	"But I will keep on using Google Drive and Gmail as you can send your work and do lots of other things. It's much easier than what we thought eventually. You can upload pictures, save them, and limit access to yourself only" (Student 29).
Network and participatory literacy	"Technology helped us with the collaborative tasks and to achieve our goals; we were able to complete them together as a team electronically" (Student 8).
Intercultural literacy	"By all this technology we have today me and my team learned a lot of things about their feelings, their thoughts and about their culture. By video calls and emails we came closer and learnt about their opinions" (Student 23).
Critical literacy	"After the first successful synchronous exchange two weeks ago, we had to do another one with another subject. We had to discuss the two different countries, Cyprus and Spain, and address some social issues. Also we had to talk more about the Cypriot NGO's challenge and the Spanish NGO's challenge and provide each other with help in solving it. This time I did the exchange only with my group via Hangouts and we focused more on our NGOs" (Student 14).

3.2. Global competences development and active citizenship

The second research question focused on the participants' interaction with technologies, and on how this interaction facilitated the development global competences and active participation in society. The analysis of data indicated that the participants' interaction with different technologies contributed to the development of various global competences, such as autonomous learning skills, flexibility, and adaptability (Council of Europe, 2016). Participants appeared to have acted autonomously and with a flexible attitude in order to adapt to the situation and overcome technical barriers. This was manifested in the fact that, independently and without direct supervision or guidance, they evaluated the different social networks that afford opportunities for interaction. By comparing and contrasting them, and analysing their benefits and drawbacks, they examined the challenges they faced before making their final selection of the most suitable social network. In many cases, participants demonstrated flexibility and adaptability using different modes of communication to sustain interaction with their partners. Table 3 summarises the students' interaction with technology and the development of global competences.

Table 3.   Development of global competences

Global competence development	Students' quotes
Autonomous learning	"I personally learned that when you have a difficulty, you can find a different way; like when we had to talk through video calls, sometimes we had a problem so we texted each other. Or, while we were making the introductory videos or the digital story, we definitely faced various difficulties, but we tried to cope with the time we were allowed in order to complete them and with the resources that were available to us" (Student 11).
Flexibility and adaptability	"We had a talk from messages and we decided to make a video call in Hangouts, but a problem emerged with our microphone and they couldn't hear us. Then we decided to make a video call from Facebook but their Internet connection was low. Eventually, we did it and we had a talk for about half an hour" (Student 19).

Most importantly, it appears that the technological mediation in this project was conducive to critical global competences, such as civic-mindedness and active citizenship. In the YES project, technology was used with a critical perspective as participants were prompted to join the 'maker movement' (Gauntlett, 2013) by co-creating innovative digital artefacts in response to current social problems (Nicolaou & Sevilla-Pavón, 2018; Sevilla-Pavón & Nicolaou, 2020), thus becoming active, engaged citizens rather than users or consumers of technology and resources (Selwyn, 2014 cited in Pangrazio, 2016). This critical engagement with technology led to the development of civic engagement in society (Godwin-Jones, 2019; O'Dowd, 2019) and civic-mindedness, as this is described in the Council of Europe's (2016) Reference Framework of Competences for Democratic Culture.

Table 4 summarises the participants' critical interaction with technology and the development of civic-mindedness.

Table 4. Development of civic-mindedness

Civic-mindedness	Students' quotes
Becoming digital 'makers' in order to improve the situation of other people in the local community	"Our business idea is an app that will help immigrants to learn Greek for free by a code that they will take by miHUB. The thought about this idea was inspired by the problem miHUB (Migrant Information Centre) had; that is the communication problem that immigrants face when they come to Cyprus. The solution that the foreign students gave to us is that we can maybe contact a Greek organization similar to ours and explain to them the problem we have" (Student 16).
Discussing what can be done to help make the community a better place	"After all we talked about our organisations' problems. Their organisation helps women and children who live in poor conditions; their organisation's problem is that there are not many people who are willing to help them. So our suggestion for a solution to their problem was to make people sensitise about their mission so they will feel how difficult it is to live in such poor conditions" (Student 17).
Discussing volunteerism and charitable activities	"Apart from this, we also discussed our NGO's social challenge and we helped each other by giving a solution to the problem. For example, our organisations were facing the same economical problem. So, they suggested to organise a festival or a charity marathon with the aim to raise money and maybe some advertising leaflets would be a good idea for people to get to know the organisation" (Student 18).
Taking action to solve environmental problems	"Our partners decided to create a product. The basic purpose of this product is to reduce plastic pollution in the world" (Student 21).
Supporting organisations addressing social issues	"Yesterday I was having my second synchronous exchange with my partner from Spain. This time, we had to discuss how different countries address the same issues. Also, we had to talk about the Cypriot NGO's challenge and the Spanish too and helping each other to solve the organisations' problems" (Student 2).

3.3. Limitations

This study yielded interesting results in response to the two research questions. However, the results are limited to the Cypriot part of the exchange. The perceptions of the participants from the Spanish university would provide further insights as to the development of digital literacies and global competence learning. In addition, even though both focus groups and reflection papers were analysed to triangulate the data, they were not exhaustive in capturing the complete picture of the learners' experiences as described in this paper. Interaction data on Google Hangouts, Google+ Communities, and email exchanges would have been valuable in recording instances of critical interaction with technology as well as digital and global competence learning.

4. Conclusions

The virtual exchange reported in this study draws attention to critical digital literacies and the potential of computer-mediated communication to provide opportunities for authentic communication and purposeful collaboration within international partnerships, with a view to responding to critical global challenges and community problem solving. In this global virtual exchange project, technology served as a crucial contextual element that related learners with other learners, with teachers, with civil society, and with resources. The sustained intercultural synchronous and asynchronous interaction and the collaborative creation of authentic digital artefacts involved the use of technology in a creative way and activated various competences, such as autonomy, flexibility, adaptability, as well as the orchestration of multimodal skills. In addition, the technological tools facilitated discussions about current societal challenges at local and global level. Through these discussions, students learned about organisations and volunteer groups that promote human rights, and shared this information with their partners to inform them and raise awareness. The participants moved beyond the functional uses of technology (Hauck, 2019) and utilised technological tools to reach out to their local communities and address local challenges through international, action-oriented, problem-solving engagement. In this project, the role of technology was to optimise the learning environment with its unique affordances. Therefore, technology was viewed through the lens of its potential to support the humanistic role of education by mediating relationships and contributing to the participants' active participation in society.

5. Acknowledgements

Portions of this manuscript are drawn from my unpublished doctoral thesis: Nicolaou (2020).

References

Ávila, J., & Pandya, J. Z. (2013). *Critical digital literacies as social praxis: Intersections and challenges. New literacies and digital epistemologies* (vol. 54). Peter Lang.

BrckaLorenz, A., & Gieser, J. (2011, November). *Global awareness and student engagement*. Association for the Study of Higher Education Annual Conference.

Brown, A. L. (1992). Design experiments: theoretical and methodological challenges in creating complex interventions in classroom settings. *The Journal of the Learning Sciences, 2*(2), 141-178. https://doi.org/10.1207/s15327809jls0202_2

Byram, M. (1997). *Teaching and assessing intercultural communicative competence*. Multilingual Matters.

Byram, M. (2008). Intercultural citizenship and foreign language education. *Recuperado el, 20*, 122-132.

Clarke, V., & Braun, V. (2017). Thematic analysis. *The Journal of Positive Psychology, 12*(3), 297-298. https://doi.org/10.1080/17439760.2016.1262613

Cohen, J. (1960). A coefficient of agreement for nominal scales. *Educational and psychological measurement, 20*, 37-46.

Collins, A. (1992). Toward a design science of education. In E. Scanlon & T. O'Shea (Eds), *New directions in educational technology* (pp. 15-22). Springer.

Common Sense Education. (2017). *Top tools for remixing*. Common Sense Education. https://www.commonsense.org/education/top-picks/top-tools-forremixing

Council of Europe. (2016). *Competences for democratic culture: living together as equals in culturally diverse democratic societies. Executive Summary*. Council of Europe Publishing.

Cushner, K., & Brennan, S. (2007). *Intercultural student teaching: a bridge to global competence*. Rowman & Littlefield Education.

Darvin, R., & Norton, B. (2014). Transnational identity and migrant language learners: the promise of digital storytelling. *Education Matters: The Journal of Teaching and Learning, 2*(1), 55-66.

Dudeney, G. (2011). Digital literacies and the language classroom. *KOTESOL Proceedings 2011*, 31-35.

Dudeney, G., & Hockly, N. (2016). Literacies, technology and language teaching. In F. Farr & L. Murray (Eds), *The Routledge handbook of language learning and technology*. (pp. 115-126). Routledge.

Dudeney, G., Hockly, N., & Pegrum, M. (2013). *Digital literacies: research and resources in language teaching*. Pearson Education Limited.

Elliott-Gower, S., & Hill, K. W. (2015). The Soliya Connect Program: two institutions' experience with virtual intercultural. *eJournal of Public Affairs*, *4*(1), 114.

Gauntlett, D. (2013). *Making is connecting*. John Wiley & Sons.

Godwin-Jones, R. (2019). Telecollaboration as an approach to developing intercultural communication competence. *Language Learning & Technology*, *23*(3), 8-28. http://hdl.handle.net/10125/44691

Hauck, M. (2019). Virtual exchange for (critical) digital literacy skills development. *European Journal of Language Policy*, *11*(2), 187-210. https://doi.org/10.3828/ejlp.2019.12

Hauck, M., & Kurek, M. (2017). Digital literacies in teacher preparation. In S. Thorne & S. May (Eds), *Language, education and technology* (3rd ed., pp. 1-13). Encyclopedia of Language and Education. Springer International Publishing. https://doi.org/10.1007/978-3-319-02237-6_22

Hauck, M., & Satar, H. M. (2018). Learning and teaching languages in technology-mediated contexts: the relevance of social presence, co-presence, participatory literacy and multimodal competence. In R. Kern & C. Develotte (Eds), *Screens and scenes: online multimodal communication and intercultural encounters: theoretical and educational perspectives*. (pp. 133-157). Routledge. https://doi.org/10.4324/9781315447124-7

Helm, F. (2013). A dialogic model for telecollaboration. *Bellaterra Journal of Teaching & Learning Language & Literature*, *6*(2), 28-48. https://doi.org/10.5565/rev/jtl3.522

Helm, F. (2014). Developing digital literacies through virtual exchange. *Elearning Papers*, *38*, 1-10.

Helm, F. (2015). The practices and challenges of telecollaboration in higher education in Europe. *Language Learning & Technology*, *19*(2), 197-217.

Jackson, J. (2011). Cultivating cosmopolitan, intercultural citizenship through critical reflection and international, experiential learning. *Language and Intercultural Communication*, *11*(2), 80-96. https://doi.org/10.1080/14708477.2011.556737

Juuti, K., & Lavonen, J. (2006). Design-based research in science education: one step towards methodology. *Nordic Studies in Science Education, 2*(2), 54-68.

Kopish, M., & Marques, W. (2020). Leveraging technology to promote global citizenship in teacher education in the United States and Brazil. *Research in Social Sciences and Technology, 5*(1), 45-69. https://doi.org/10.46303/ressat.05.01.3

Kurek, M., & Turula, A. (2014). Digital autonomy-wishful thinking or reality? On teacher attitudes to Web 2.0 tools. *Attitudes to technology in ESL/EFL pedagogy*, 112-28.

Lambert, J. (2013). *Digital storytelling: capturing lives, creating community.* Routledge.

Mansilla, V. B., Jackson, A., & Jacobs, I. H. (2013). Educating for global competence: learning redefined for an interconnected world. In H. Jacobs (Ed.), *Mastering global literacy, contemporary perspectives* (pp. 5-27). Solution Tree.

Mishra, P., & Koehler, M. J. (2006). Technological pedagogical content knowledge: a framework for teacher knowledge. *Teachers College Record, 108*(6), 1017-1054.

Nicolaou, A. (2020). *The affordances of virtual exchange for developing global competence and active citizenship in content-based language learning.* Unpublished doctoral thesis. Trinity College Dublin, the University of Dublin.

Nicolaou, A., & Sevilla-Pavón, A. (2016). Exploring telecollaboration through the lens of university students. In S. Jager, M. Kurek & B. O'Rourke (Eds), *New directions in telecollaborative research and practice: selected papers from the second conference on telecollaboration in higher education* (pp. 113-120). Research-publishing.net. https://doi.org/10.14705/rpnet.2016.telecollab2016.497

Nicolaou, A., & Sevilla-Pavón, A. (2017). Redesigning a telecollaboration project towards an ecological constructivist approach. In *Call in context, proceedings, Berkeley, University of California, 7 - 9 July 2017* (pp. 589-597). http://call2017.language.berkeley.edu/wp-content/uploads/2017/07/CALL2017_proceedings.pdf?

Nicolaou, A., & Sevilla-Pavón, A. (2018). Expanding a telecollaborative project through social entrepreneurship. In J. Colpaert, A. Aerts & F. Cornillie (Eds), *CALL your DATA: proceedings* (pp. 295-302). University of Antwerp. https://www.call2018.org/wp-content/uploads/2018/07/proceedings-CALL-2018.pdf

O'Dowd, R. (2007). (Ed.). *Online intercultural exchange: an introduction for foreign language teachers.* Multilingual Matters.

O'Dowd, R. (2016). Emerging trends and new directions in telecollaborative learning. *Calico Journal, 33*(3), 291-310. https://doi.org/10.1558/cj.v33i3.30747

O'Dowd, R. (2018). From telecollaboration to virtual exchange: state-of-the-art and the role of UNICollaboration in moving forward. *Journal of Virtual Exchange, 1*, 1-23. https://doi.org/10.14705/rpnet.2018.jve.1

O'Dowd, R. (2019). A transnational model of virtual exchange for global citizenship education. *Language Teaching, 53*(4), 477-490. https://doi.org/10.1017/S0261444819000077

O'Rourke, B., & Stickler, U. (2017). Synchronous communication technologies for language learning: promise and challenges in research and pedagogy. *Language Learning in Higher Education, 7*(1), 1-20. https://doi.org/10.1515/cercles-2017-0009

Ørngreen, R. (2015, June). Reflections on design-based research. In *IFIP Working Conference on Human Work Interaction Design* (pp. 20-38). Springer. https://doi.org/10.1007/978-3-319-27048-7_2

Pangrazio, L. (2016). Reconceptualising critical digital literacy. *Discourse: Studies in the cultural politics of education, 37*(2), 163-174. https://doi.org/10.1080/01596306.2014.942836

Pegrum, M., Dudeney, G., & Hockly, N. (2018). Digital literacies revisited. *European Journal of Applied Linguistics and TEFL, 7*(2), 3-24.

Piccardo, A. P. E., & North, B. (2019). *The action-oriented approach: a dynamic vision of language education*. Multilingual Matters.

Prensky, M. (2001). Digital natives, digital immigrants. Part 1. *On the Horizon, 9*(5), 1-6. https://doi.org/10.1108/10748120110424816

Robin, B. (2009). Digital storytelling: a powerful technology tool for the 21st century classroom. *Journal Theory into Practice, 47*(3), 220-228. https://doi.org/10.1080/00405840802153916

Selwyn, N. (2014). *Distrusting educational technology: critical questions for changing times*. Routledge.

Sevilla-Pavón, A., & Nicolaou, A. (2019). Business English 3.0: hands-on online and virtual collaboration tasks. *Granada: Editorial Comares. Education in the digital age* (pp. 170-187). IGI Global.

Sevilla-Pavón, A., & Nicolaou, A. (2020). Artefact co-construction in virtual exchange: 'Youth Entrepreneurship for Society'. *Computer Assisted Language Learning*, 1-26. https://doi.org/10.1080/09588221.2020.1825096

Stemler, S. (2001). An overview of content analysis. Practical Assement. *Research and Evaluation, 7*, 124-130.

Tapscott, D. (1999). Educating the net generation. *Educational leadership, 56*(5), 6-11.

Van Lier, L. (2004). The semiotics and ecology of language learning. *Utbildning & Demokrati, 13*(3), 79-103.

Van Lier, L. (2008). Agency in the classroom. In J. P. Lantolf & M. E. Poehner (Eds), *Sociocultural theory and the teaching of second languages* (pp. 163-186). Equinox.

Van Lier, L. (2010). The ecology of language learning: practice to theory, theory to practice. *Procedia-Social and Behavioral Sciences, 3*, 2-6. https://doi.org/10.1016/j.sbspro.2010.07.005

Vinagre, M. (2016). Developing key competences for life-long learning through virtual collaboration: teaching ICT in English as a medium of instruction. In C. Wang & L. Winstead (Eds), *Handbook of research on foreign language education in the digital age* (pp. 170-187). IGI Global. https://doi.org/10.4018/978-1-5225-0177-0.ch008

# 7 The integration of embodied learning in a language learning classroom: conclusions from a qualitative analysis

Panagiotis Kosmas[1]

Abstract

Embodied Learning (EL) is now an emerging teaching paradigm that takes into consideration the impact of bodily movements into the learning process. This paradigm, in combination with movement-based technologies, provides strategies and methods for delivering a more engaged and interactive lesson. Following previous empirical evidence, this study presents the results of an educational intervention, based on EL, in the context of language learning in mainstream elementary schools. The study aims to examine whether this practice would improve students' language performance and enhance their engagement in, and motivation for, learning a language. One hundred and eighteen (N=118) elementary students and six teachers were involved in this investigation. Data were collected from video recordings of 12 intervention sessions in the classroom. The analysis of video recordings provided rich information about the engagement of the students in the classroom during the sessions. It revealed that the EL practice enabled students to actively engage in the lesson, increasing their motivation and participation. Finally, the manuscript discusses the use of such an EL approach in language learning and teaching.

Keywords: embodied cognition, embodied learning, elementary education, language learning, qualitative analysis.

1. Cyprus University of Technology, Limassol, Cyprus; panayiotis.kosmas@cut.ac.cy; https://orcid.org/0000-0003-3079-5556

How to cite: Kosmas, P. (2021). The integration of embodied learning in a language learning classroom: conclusions from a qualitative analysis. In S. Papadima-Sophocleous, E. Kakoulli Constantinou & C. N. Giannikas (Eds), *Tertiary education language learning: a collection of research* (pp. 133-149). Research-publishing.net. https://doi.org/10.14705/rpnet.2021.51.1258

Chapter 7

1. Introduction

The existing literature in the area of EL demonstrates that the integration of movement could improve students' academic and emotional performance (Kosmas, Ioannou, & Retalis, 2017; Kosmas, Ioannou, & Zaphiris, 2018). The EL framework points out the inseparable link between brain and body, and offers alternative practices and solutions on how bodily movements can be integrated into our teaching methodologies. This link between brain-body has been investigated by many researchers in different disciplines, such as in the areas of cognition, psychology, and linguistics, among others. The focus of the research was related to the value of the involvement of the physical body in the learning process and how this involvement can change people's learning and cognitive performance (Wilson, 2002).

Thus, over the last decades, EL has evolved as one paradigm of contemporary teaching and learning practice (Foglia & Wilson, 2013). In that way, the concept of EL plays a significant part in the area of educational research intending to examine whether this practice affects students' overall performance (Lindgren & Johnson-Glenberg, 2013). The use of technology is also one thing that we have to consider when we talk about EL. Technologies that require movement (e.g. Kinect, leap motion, etc.) provide solutions with regard to the integration of the EL approach into the classroom. In this context, students can take part in the whole learning process, engage in a more meaningful way in learning, and have direct physical interaction with the learning material (Chandler & Tricot, 2015).

Despite the recent growing interest in EL in educational settings, empirical research focusing on qualitative data in real school settings is limited (Kosmas & Zaphiris, 2018). The contribution of this research is to provide an insight into how students react in these EL conditions, since video recording can capture all students' behaviour during the intervention sessions. It also provides one example of how teachers can integrate or introduce EL into their teaching practice.

Specifically, the EL intervention described in this study shows empirically how technology can support the EL approach in the context of first language acquisition (L1). The educational interventions were carried out in real language learning classrooms to examine:

- students' engagement and motivation in participating in this type of learning; and

- the factors which can affect the delivery of EL.

2. Theoretical background

2.1. Embodied Cognition (EC)

The involvement of the physical body in the cognitive and learning process is part of the theoretical framework of EC. The theoretical framework of EC has gained attention over the last two decades (Fugate, Macrine, & Cipriano, 2019). It emphasises the relationship between sensory-motor processes and abstract cognitive processes (Duijzer et al., 2019) and claims that the body plays a significant part in cognitive mechanisms (Wilson, 2002). It is also believed that the connection between body-mind comes true when physical interaction and movement are linked with learning content (Ayala, Mendívil, Salinas, & Rios, 2013).

Although EC theory is in its early stages, there is a huge amount of multidisciplinary and interdisciplinary literature around the implications of EC in many areas, including education. The literature offers significant recommendations in terms of the use of EC in educational practice. One such recommendation is the EL framework, which can enhance educational practice offering new strategies and methods to make students' learning experience effective and meaningful (Shapiro & Stolz, 2019).

2.2. Empirical evidence of EL in language acquisition

There is a large and diverse body of literature on the significance of EC theory for language learning and teaching. Previous research emphasised the need for more active learning experiences where students can use their bodily movements to understand the material that is being taught (Cassar & Jang, 2010; Kosmas, Ioannou, & Retalis, 2018; Kosmas, Ioannou, & Zaphiris, 2018). Scholars in this area suggest that the learner's ability to comprehend a language relates to the ability to simulate the action involved in the meaning (Fugate et al., 2019).

Focusing on a language learning context, many studies have explored how gestures or movements can affect specific areas of language learning, like phonological awareness and reading (Moritz et al., 2013), while some other studies have shown the impact of movement' integration for language development and comprehension. Findings from the study of Booth et al. (2014) have revealed that physical activity has a positive impact on student academic performance, while the study of Chaddock-Heyman et al. (2014), has demonstrated that embodied interaction improves neural connectivity within the brain. Along the same lines, other studies in this area have pointed out the link between movement and specific words demonstrating that children acquire new vocabulary better when they connect a movement with a word (Kosmas & Zaphiris, 2019a). Moreover, Glenberg (2010) highlighted that memory and perception are affected by movement, while Bokosmaty, Mavilidi, and Paas (2017) have claimed that physical movements enhance learners' memory by expanding their working memory capacity to deal with complex learning tasks. Other studies have demonstrated the impact of EL on the students' verbal information (Chang et al., 2013), others on students' recall of information (Gao et al., 2013) and others on students' second language comprehension (Lee et al., 2012).

More recently, in the same context, some studies have also revealed the potential of such EL activities for students' performance and memory. The results of previous research showed important considerations regarding the positive impact of physical activity during learning. For example, Schmidt et al. (2019), examining 104 elementary school children's performance, have concluded that children enjoy physically active learning scenarios more than the sedentary. Additionally, Kosmas and Zaphiris (2019a) have revealed significant gains in students' academic achievements in language acquisition and documented improvements in students' emotional engagement. Finally, the qualitative analysis of 52 elementary students in EL conditions indicated that EL interactions facilitated collaboration between students by engaging them in learning activities physically and emotionally (Kosmas & Zaphiris, 2019b).

Outside of language learning, a huge number of studies have shown that EL approaches enhanced students' learning outcomes in mathematics and science (Abrahamson, 2013; Chen & Fang, 2014; Kellman & Massey, 2013). The study of Mavilidi et al. (2018) working with 120 pre-school children in different groups, has revealed that children in the physical activity group performed better than children in all other conditions. A recent work by Ioannou, Georgiou, Ioannou, and Johnson (2019) investigating students' learning and perceptions of technology integration in two different contexts (high-embodied and low-embodied), revealed improved learning gains and more positive attitudes towards technology integration, for the students in both conditions. Also, Voillot, Bevilacqua, Chevrier, and Eliot (2019) highlighted the important role of movement-based digital interfaces for empowering children and emphasised the need for active early childhood education.

Taking all the above into consideration, there is important empirical evidence for the use of movement in achieving better learning gains in different language learning contexts, such as first language acquisition, second language acquisition, foreign language acquisition, etc. What has not yet been investigated is the behaviour (e.g. engagement, participation, motivation) of the students in an EL environment that combines the teaching of language with embodied technology in real contexts.

3. Research design

The analysis of this study focused on qualitative data. A qualitative approach was used in this study to analyse the video data from 12 consecutive intervention sessions in the classroom. In terms of having and analysing qualitative data from students' activities, researchers claimed that capturing classroom dynamics makes it possible to analyse exactly what goes on between the students and the teacher (Raca & Dillenbourg, 2014). Video data provide a clearer picture of the students' behaviour during the sessions and make possible the holistic view of the whole research process (Jacobs, Kawanaka, & Stigler, 1999). The cycle of coding and analysis of video data includes watching, coding, and analysing the data, with the goal of transforming the video images into objective and verifiable information (Jacobs et al., 1999).

3.1. Participants

A total of 118 elementary classroom students from two different schools were involved in the study and participated in a three-month intervention in order to complete 12 EL sessions in the classroom. Students attended mainstream public schools in Cyprus and the average age of students was 7.6 years old. The students' mother language was Greek, and the intervention took place in L1 lessons in first and second-grade classes. In the study, six primary school teachers were involved in the intervention.

3.2. The interventions in the classroom

As mentioned earlier, the intervention sessions were designed, organised, and prepared based on an EL perspective. All the activities were aimed at engaging students in an EL environment, where they could move while learning a new vocabulary. To achieve this, we have designed a movement-based intervention, based on the idea of EL, in order to enhance the vocabulary and language acquisition of first and second graders using the strengths of their bodily movements (for a detailed analysis of the movement-based intervention see the work of Kosmas & Zaphiris, 2019a). In a nutshell, the intervention included short video presentations combining bodily movements with specific words. The video presentations included in total 80 movement-words accompanied by easy steps to be followed by students. All the sessions were designed to be implemented collaboratively in the classroom with increased difficulty across the sessions.

All the intervention sessions were delivered once a week over three months during L1 lessons. Students completed 12 courses of 30 minute duration each. The video presentations had clear visual instructions (using animations) on how to perform each movement, each of which represented one specific word. Students engaged in an EL environment using their bodies to learn and acquire new vocabulary. Figure 1 presents some episodes from the EL intervention session in the classroom.

Figure 1. Students in 'action': episodes from interventions in a language classroom

3.3. Qualitative dataset

All classroom sessions were video recorded. The video data were used to yield information about the physical engagement and interaction of the students and to understand how EL worked in the classroom.

Notably, as Garcez, Duarte, and Eisenberg (2011) stated, video recording, as a data collection strategy, is a rich source of information, especially in research with children. The cameras were positioned in two different places in the classroom and captured most of the students' movements. In the end, 40 minutes of material were recorded for each classroom per session. The video material was

Chapter 7

intended to yield rich information about the physical engagement and interaction of the students and to show just how EL worked in the classroom. Collecting video material also allowed us to view what users actually did in the learning setting, capturing behaviour that would otherwise have gone unreported. Indeed, video data gave us opportunities to capture aspects that may go unnoticed during the intervention session. Many episodes of video data gave us a whole picture of students' performance and engagement in the classroom.

4.   Findings

4.1.   Students' language learning performance

Based on the analysis of video recordings of 12 intervention sessions, it seems that students enjoyed the EL activities and managed to improve their L1 language skills. The fact that students were motivated to participate in all the activities using technology enabled them to perform successfully in all the in-class activities and improve their skills. The EL practices facilitated the delivery of the lesson since all students participated actively in the activities following the instructions of the teacher.

Specifically, analysing some video episodes and focusing on students' reactions and discussions at the end of interventions, students improved their language skills in terms of new vocabulary acquisition and comprehension of new words. From the collected data, it is obvious that children learned some new words which are significantly important at this stage of their education (first and second grade). What has emerged from the recordings is that students can memorise new words easily when those are linked with a movement. This assumption is explained from the fact that every time that students have been asked to recall one new word, they imitated the specific movement of this word. At the end, students managed to connect most of the new words with the respective movement which is a kind of proof that EL helped them to develop a new way in words' understanding.

4.2. Students' behaviour and factors for implementing EL in the classroom

The analysis of the video data was employed according to the procedure described in Barron and Engle (2007), as follows: (1) guiding questions and indexing (field notes), (2) macro-level coding, (3) narrative summaries, (4) categorisation of the themes, (5) final coding, and (6) discussion of emerged categories.

Video analysis revealed many important insights into how EL can be implemented in authentic language classroom environments. As derived from video data, the essential point is that this intervention enabled all students to participate actively in learning and to improve their performance in language. Data from video recording revealed that the effective implementation of EL in the classroom is based on five factors: (1) the teacher's role, (2) the technology used for EL purposes, (3) collaboration between students, (4) classroom setting, and (5) organisation of in-class activities.

First, an important factor in implementing successful EL interventions in class-wide settings is the teacher, whose participation is critical at the beginning. The teacher must provide clear guidelines for children on how they can complete the EL activities. These guidelines should be repeated if necessary. Encouraging children to continue is also very important, especially during the first interventions. In subsequent sessions, the role of the teacher is more instructive. The teacher should help children where needed and intervene only when children find it challenging to progress. For instance, observing an episode in the classroom, the teacher encouraged students to continue their activity and gave them some guidelines, as showcased in the following information flow example.

> **Teacher**: Come on, guys; follow the instructions! [Points to a particular area on the screen that contains the instructions.]
> **Student 1**: And now? What will I do now?

Chapter 7

> **Teacher**: Look at the screen [points to the specific area on the screen]. The guy (animation) says that you should raise your left hand.
> **Student 1**: [Follows the instruction]
> **Teacher**: Good job! Great!
> **Student 1**: And now?
> **Teacher**: Continue.... [Points again on screen]. Be careful of what the animation says.
> **Student 1**: Ah, ok...

The classroom setting is also significant for the development of interventions. Children need to have the space to move about the classroom without any obstacles. They need to feel comfortable and familiar with the space so they can participate actively throughout the process. Students must have easy access to the screen so they do not miss the instructions. For example, observing some children during the session, we realised that the children in the back rows of the classroom had no direct access to the screen, and could not follow the instructions, as shown in the example below.

> **Student 2**: What should we do now? I don't know!
> **Student 3**: Look at the screen!
> **Student 2**: [student tries to read the instructions]
> **Teacher**: Come on! Do you see what the animation is doing?
> **Student 2**: No, the screen is far away from me! I can't see!
> **Student 4**: And now? I don't see the animation's movements very well!

Technology also plays an essential role in successful implementation of EL in the classroom. Everything should be ready and organised in advance so as not to waste time or create confusion when the intervention starts. The more playful the activities, the more kids like them. Technology encourages children to participate in the learning process, but when the technology does not work, it makes the situation difficult and the classroom experience more chaotic. Due to the physicality of EL learning activities, the technological tools that teachers use should make the classroom physical and flexible. Finally, activities need to change from session to session because children get bored quickly. Each new activity must build on the last so that children are motivated to continue, as in the example below.

> **Student 5**: Oh! This is a new movement!
> **Student 6**: Yep.... It's difficult! I am not sure if I will manage it!
> **Student 5**: [Tries to do the movement showing the way to his classmate]
> **Student 7**: I did it! Great!
> **Student 5**: I did it too! Cool!
> **Student 6**: Look at this [shows the animation's movement and laughs].
> **Student 5**: Let's try then!

As stated by Kosmas and Zaphiris (2019b), "it is also important [...] to cultivate an atmosphere of cooperation in the classroom because [... interventions often require teamwork...] it was often observed during the intervention that some children were encouraged to continue by their classmates. At other times, when students didn't understand [the] instructions, they followed their classmates in order to advance to the next step" (p. 192), as in the example below.

> **Student 8**: What is this?
> **Student 9**: What? It's easy! [Tries to perform the movement]
> **Student 8**: [Observe what his classmate is doing]
> **Student 9**: You see? I did it! Do you see it? [Perform the movement again]. Did you understand?
> **Student 8**: [tries one more time to perform the movement]
> **Student 9**: Bravo! That's it!

Given the positive results from this investigation, I can argue categorically that EL-driven technologies should be integrated into the language learning classroom. Figure 2 below visualises the pattern of the implementation of EL in class-wide classroom context, highlighting the five factors of such implementation. These factors are the teacher's role, the use of technology, collaboration between students, the set-up of the classroom, and the type of in-class activities.

Figure 2. Essential factors for the implementation of EL in a language classroom

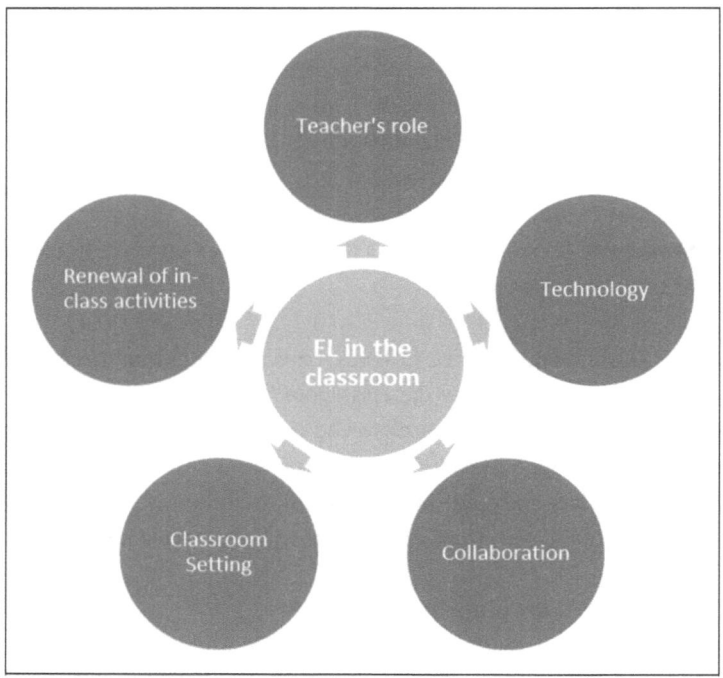

5. Discussion

This study, focusing on the analysis of qualitative data collected from the video recording, provides insights for the use of EL in a language learning environment. The video data provide more evidence of how the body can be used in educational interventions, taking into consideration the interaction and engagement of students during the intervention sessions. This type of practice in teaching, known as EL, encourages students to engage in learning activities both physically and emotionally. At the same time, this specific experiment offers a paradigm for movement-based language lessons, especially for first and second graders.

This investigation offers a paradigm based on the EL idea and claims that the EL can create an enjoyable collaborative environment in the classroom. All students were motivated during the sessions, enjoyed the process, and were willing to participate in more EL activities. EL and movement-based activities enable students to take action into the learning process and give them the opportunity to interact with the learning material. It is also suggested, based on the qualitative dataset analysed, that the implementation of EL in the classroom is based on five essential factors: the teacher's role in the classroom, the type and the use of technology, the opportunities for collaboration between students, the classroom orchestration, and the type of in-class activities. The consideration of the above factor is critical for the effective implementation of an educational intervention based on EL principles. Furthermore, this intervention presented in the study gives an example of how language teachers can enrich the teaching of language lessons by including aspects of bodily movements and physical interaction. The results of this research are in line with other research studies which believe that an embodied view of teaching and learning can improve students' language readiness and acquisition (Krog & Krüger, 2011).

In closing, given the positive results from this investigation, we can argue that the EL approach with the use of technology can be integrated into classroom language learning curricula. By doing so, teachers will have the opportunity to boost children's language skills in an enriched sensorimotor environment, which can positively impact not only their academic performance but also their engagement in the process.

6. Acknowledgements

I would like to thank all students and teachers who participated voluntarily in these sessions.

Chapter 7

References

Abrahamson, D. (2013). Building educational activities for understanding: an elaboration on the embodied-design framework and its epistemic grounds. *International Journal of Child-Computer Interaction, 2*(1), 1-16. https://doi.org/10.1016/j.ijcci.2014.07.002

Ayala, N. A. R., Mendívil, E. G., Salinas, P., & Rios, H. (2013). Kinesthetic learning applied to mathematics using kinect. *Procedia Computer Science, 25*, 131-135. https://doi.org/10.1016/j.procs.2013.11.016

Barron, B., & Engle, R. A. (2007). Analyzing data derived from video records. In S. J. Derry (Ed.), *Guidelines for video research in education: recommendations from an expert panel* (pp. 24-33). Data Research and Development Center. https://drdc.uchicago.edu/what/video-research-guidelines.pdf

Bokosmaty, S., Mavilidi, M. F., & Paas, F. (2017). Effects of making and observing movements with interactive geometry software on learning geometry. *Computers & Education, 113*, 313-326. https://doi.org/10.1016/j.compedu.2017.06.008

Booth, J. N., Leary, S. D., Joinson, C., Ness, A. R., Tomporowski, P. D., Boyle, J. M., & Reilly, J. J. (2014). Associations between objectively measured physical activity and academic attainment in adolescents from a UK cohort. *British journal of sports medicine, 48*(3), 265-270. https://doi.org/10.1136/bjsports-2013-092334

Cassar, A., & Jang, E. (2010). Investigating the effects of a game-based approach in teaching word recognition and spelling to students with reading disabilities and attention deficits. *Australian Journal of Learning Difficulties, 15*(2), 193-211. https://doi.org/10.1080/19404151003796516

Chaddock-Heyman, L., Erickson, K. I., Holtrop, J. L., Voss, M. W., Pontifex, M. B., Raine, L. B., Hillman, C. H., & Kramer, A. F. (2014). Aerobic fitness is associated with greater white matter integrity in children. *Frontiers in human neuroscience, 8*, 584. https://doi.org/10.3389/fnhum.2014.00584

Chandler, P., & Tricot, A. (2015). Mind your body: the essential role of body movements in children's learning. *Educational Psychology Review, 27*(3), 365-370. https://doi.org/10.1007/s10648-015-9333-3

Chang, C. Y., Chien, Y. T., Chiang, C. Y., Lin, M. C., & Lai, H. C. (2013). Embodying gesture-based multimedia to improve learning. *British Journal of Educational Technology, 44*(1), E5-E9. https://doi.org/10.1111/j.1467-8535.2012.01311.x

Chen, N., & Fang, W. (2014). Gesture-based technologies for enhancing learning. In R. Huang, Kinshuk, N.-S. Chen & Editors (Eds), *The new development of technology enhanced learning. Concept, research and best practices* (pp. 95-112). Springer Berlin Heidelberg. https://doi.org/10.1007/978-3-642-38291-8_6

Duijzer, C., Van den Heuvel-Panhuizen, M., Veldhuis, M., Doorman, M., & Leseman, P. (2019). Embodied learning environments for graphing motion: a systematic literature review. *Educational Psychology Review, 31*(3), 597-629. https://doi.org/10.1007/s10648-019-09471-7

Foglia, L., & Wilson, R. A. (2013). Embodied cognition. *Wiley Interdisciplinary Reviews: Cognitive Science, 4*(3), 319-325. https://doi.org/10.1002/wcs.1226

Fugate, J. M., Macrine, S. L., & Cipriano, C. (2019). The role of embodied cognition for transforming learning. *International Journal of School & Educational Psychology, 7*(4), 274-288. https://doi.org/10.1080/21683603.2018.1443856

Gao, Z., Hannan, P., Xiang, P., Stodden, D. F., & Valdez, V. E. (2013). Video game–based exercise, Latino children's physical health, and academic achievement. *American journal of preventive medicine, 44*(3), 240-246. https://doi.org/10.1016/j.amepre.2012.11.023

Garcez, A., Duarte, R., & Eisenberg, Z. (2011). Production and analysis of video recordings in qualitative research. *Educação e Pesquisa, 37*(2), 249-261.

Glenberg, A. M. (2010). Embodiment as a unifying perspective for psychology. *Wiley Interdisciplinary Reviews: Cognitive Science, 1*(4), 586-596. https://doi.org/10.1002/wcs.55

Ioannou, M., Georgiou, Y., Ioannou, A., & Johnson, M. (2019). On the understanding of students' learning and perceptions of technology integration in low-and high-embodied group learning. *Repository of the International Society of Learning Sciences.* https://repository.isls.org//handle/1/1582

Jacobs, J. K., Kawanaka, T., & Stigler, J. W. (1999). Integrating qualitative and quantitative approaches to the analysis of video data on classroom teaching. *International Journal of Educational Research, 31*(8), 717-724. https://doi.org/10.1016/s0883-0355(99)00036-1

Kellman, P. J., & Massey, C. M. (2013). Perceptual learning, cognition, and expertise. *The psychology of learning and motivation, 58,* 117-165. https://doi.org/10.1016/b978-0-12-407237-4.00004-9

Kosmas, P., Ioannou A., & Retalis S. (2017). Using embodied learning technology to advance motor performance of children with special educational needs and motor impairments. In É. Lavoué, H. Drachsler, K. Verbert, J. Broisin, & M. Pérez-Sanagustín (Eds), *Data driven approaches in digital education. EC-TEL 2017. Lecture Notes in Computer Science, vol 10474.* Springer. https://doi.org/10.1007/978-3-319-66610-5_9

Kosmas, P., Ioannou, A., & Retalis, S. (2018). Moving bodies to moving minds: a study of the use of motion-based games in special education. *TechTrends, 62*(6), 594-601. https://doi.org/10.1007/s11528-018-0294-5

Kosmas, P., Ioannou, A., & Zaphiris, P. (2018). Implementing embodied learning in the classroom: effects on children's memory and language skills. *Educational Media International, 56*(1), 59-74. https://doi.org/10.1080/09523987.2018.1547948

Kosmas, P., & Zaphiris, P. (2018). Embodied cognition and its implications in education: an overview of recent literature. World Academy of Science, Engineering and Technology, International Science Index 139. *International Journal of Social, Behavioral, Educational, Economic, Business and Industrial Engineering, 12*(7), 946-952.

Kosmas, P., & Zaphiris, P. (2019a). Words in action: investigating students' language acquisition and emotional performance through embodied learning. *Innovation in Language Learning and Teaching, 14*(4), 317-332. https://doi.org/10.1080/17501229.2019.1607355

Kosmas, P. & Zaphiris P. (2019b). Embodied interaction in language learning: enhancing students' collaboration and emotional engagement. In D. Lamas, F. Loizides, L. Nacke, H. Petrie, M. Winckler, & P. Zaphiris (Eds), *Human-computer interaction – INTERACT 2019. Lecture Notes in Computer Science* (vol 11747). Springer. https://doi.org/10.1007/978-3-030-29384-0_11

Krog, S., & Krüger, D. (2011). Movement programmes as a means to learning readiness. *South African Journal for Research in Sport, Physical Education and Recreation, 33*(3), 73-87.

Lee, W., Huang, C., Wu, C., Huang, S., & Chen, G. (2012). The effects of using embodied interactions to improve learning performance. In *2012 IEEE 12th International Conference on Advanced Learning Technologies (ICALT), July 4–6 2012* (pp.557-559).

Lindgren, R., & Johnson-Glenberg, M. (2013). Emboldened by embodiment six precepts for research on embodied learning and mixed reality. *Educational Researcher, 42*(8), 445-452. https://doi.org/10.3102/0013189x13511661

Mavilidi, M. F., Okely, A., Chandler, P., Domazet, S. L., & Paas, F. (2018). Immediate and delayed effects of integrating physical activity into preschool children's learning of numeracy skills. *Journal of Experimental Child Psychology, 166*, 502-519. https://doi.org/10.1016/j.jecp.2017.09.009

Moritz, C., Yampolsky, S., Papadelis, G., Thomson, J., & Wolf, M. (2013). Links between early rhythm skills, musical training, and phonological awareness. *Reading and Writing, 26*(5), 739-769. https://doi.org/10.1007/s11145-012-9389-0

Raca, M., & Dillenbourg, P. (2014, November). Holistic analysis of the classroom. In *Proceedings of the 2014 ACM workshop on Multimodal Learning Analytics Workshop and Grand Challenge* (pp. 13-20). https://doi.org/10.1145/2666633.2666636

Schmidt, M., Benzing, V., Wallman-Jones, A., Mavilidi, M. F., Lubans, D. R., & Paas, F. (2019). Embodied learning in the classroom: effects on primary school children's attention and foreign language vocabulary learning. *Psychology of sport and exercise, 43*, 45-54. https://doi.org/10.1016/j.psychsport.2018.12.017

Shapiro, L., & Stolz, S. A. (2019). Embodied cognition and its significance for education. *Theory and Research in Education, 17*(1), 19-39. https://doi.org/10.1177/1477878518822149

Voillot, M., Bevilacqua, F., Chevrier, J., & Eliot, C. (2019, June). Exploring embodied learning for early childhood education. In *Proceedings of the 18th ACM International Conference on Interaction Design and Children* (pp. 747-750). https://doi.org/10.1145/3311927.3325347

Wilson, M. (2002). Six views of embodied cognition. *Psychonomic Bulletin & Review, 9*(4), 625-636. https://doi.org/10.3758/bf03196322

8. The pragmatic functions and the interpretations of the particle 'taha' (τάχα) in classroom discourse in the Cypriot-Greek dialect: the emergence of a new function

Fotini Efthimiou[1]

Abstract

This paper aims to present the pragmatic functions and the interpretations of 'taha' (τάχα) (a very commonly used particle in oral Cypriot-Greek interactions) as it is used in classroom discourse. The present study collected and analysed data from a three hour recording of the participants' speech, and isolated 32 critical episodes that included 'taha'. Students were also asked to note the functions of 'taha' through the use of a questionnaire, and to interpret its functions through a discussion. Following the pragmatic analysis proposed by Tsiplakou and Papapetrou (2020), the current research concluded that the basic meaning of 'taha' ('supposedly/allegedly') may perform several pragmatic functions, depending on the context. Among others, 'taha' functions as a pragmatic marker of (1) dissociation from the associated implicatures, (2) dissociation from the propositional content, (3) request for clarifications, and (4) a hedging device. In addition, 'taha' sometimes works as a pragmatic marker of emphasis to the propositional content, a function that has not been reported in the bibliography so far.

Keywords: Cypriot-Greek 'taha', pragmatic functions, oral interactions.

1. Cyprus University of Technology, Limassol, Cyprus; fotini.efthimiou@cut.ac.cy; https://orcid.org/0000-0003-4839-518X

How to cite: Efthimiou, F. (2021). The pragmatic functions and the interpretations of the particle 'taha' (τάχα) in classroom discourse in the Cypriot-Greek dialect: the emergence of a new function. In S. Papadima-Sophocleous, E. Kakoulli Constantinou & C. N. Giannikas (Eds), *Tertiary education language learning: a collection of research* (pp. 151-166). Research-publishing.net. https://doi.org/10.14705/rpnet.2021.51.1259

Chapter 8

1. Introduction

The aim of this paper is to present the pragmatic functions and the interpretations of 'taha' (τάχα) ('supposedly/allegedly') as it is used in classroom discourse (Cazden, 1988, pp. 53-79), in the programme 'Greek for academic purposes', where participants used the Cypriot-Greek dialect.

Based on the above, this paper presents initially the lexical entry of 'taha' in six dictionaries and then the relevant research on it. Next, the phenomenon of language change is presented briefly.

'Taha' (τάχα) ('allegedly/supposedly') is very frequent in oral use in the Cypriot-Greek dialect, especially by teenagers (Tsiplakou & Papapetrou, 2020). From a pragmatic point of view, 'taha' is considered as a particle (Pavlidou, 1989, p. 327) or as a pragmatic marker (Tsiplakou & Papapetrou, 2020). In Modern Greek dictionaries, 'taha' is an adverb meaning 'supposedly/allegedly' used by a speaker who considers the content of a statement as non-real. It is used in narrations, reported speech, questions, and declaratives (Charalambakis, 2014, p. 1566; Institute of Modern Greek Studies, 2003, p. 1326; Mpampiniotis, 2002, p. 1744). It also appears as an adjective 'taha mou' (τάχα μου) (fake) (Institute of Modern Greek Studies, 2003, p. 1326), and 'ton taha' (τον τάχα) (someone who pretends to be important or magnificent) (Mpampiniotis, 2002, p. 1744), while in other cases it adds an ironic meaning to 'allegedly/supposedly'. In some contexts, 'taha' expresses a speaker's query or interest (Charalambakis, 2014, p. 1566; Institute of Modern Greek Studies, 2003, p. 1326; Mpampiniotis, 2002, p. 1744), while elsewhere it is equivalent to 'perhaps'/'maybe' (ίσως) (Charalambakis, 2014, p. 1566; Institute of Modern Greek Studies, 2003, p. 1326).

'Taha' also appears as 'tahates' (τάχατες) or 'tahamou' (τάχα μου). Triantaphyllides (1978, as cited in Pavlidou, 1989, p. 327) in his grammar calls a set of little words in Modern Greek including 'taha' hesitation adverbs, and claims that their function can be accomplished by the conjunctions 'μη', 'μήπως;' (can it be that...?/ by any chance?), while Tzartzanos (1953, as cited in Pavlidou, 1989, p. 327) calls 'taha' a particle, which refers to something that is imaginary.

Cypriot-Greek dictionaries (Yiangoullis, 2009, p. 464; Yiangoullis, 2014, p. 532) treat 'taha' mainly as an adverb, meaning 'allegedly/supposedly', or ascribe to it the meanings of 'forsooth', 'apparently', 'lest', 'as thought' (Papaggelou, 2001). It is worth mentioning that in many Cypriot-Greek dictionaries (Lexicography of the Cypriot dialect, database[2]; Hadjipieris & Kapatas, 2015; Petrides, 2016; Hadjioannou, 2000; Yiangoullis, 2002), the lexical entry of 'taha' and its variations are absent.

1.1. Literature review

There is little literature concerning 'taha' in both Standard Greek and the Cypriot-Greek dialect. Pavlidou (1989, pp. 316, 318), disagreeing with Triantaphyllides (1978), states that not all the members of this set of linguistic items (including 'taha') express hesitation on the part of the speaker, adding that those items differ in a syntactic, pragmatic, and semantic point of view. Adopting the terminology 'particle', suggested by Tzartzanos (1953), Pavlidou (1989) points out that 'taha' has a metacommunicative function as a result of its semantic effect by which it "reverses the truth value of the sentence" (p. 327).

Studying 'taha' in Modern Greek informal conversations and written prose, Ifantidou (2000, pp. 119-144) states that when 'taha' is used with its evidential meaning ('maybe', 'it seems', 'apparently'[3]) the speaker's commitment to the proposition expressed is reduced. However, in some contexts, 'taha' is used as an expression of implicature. Furthermore, she presents the account of Pavlidou (1989), who states that (1) rather than speaker's hesitation, 'taha' expresses an indirect and subjective certainty; (2) in interrogatives, 'taha' turns a genuine request for information into a rhetorical question and, consequently, it functions as an indirect assertion that the action which is described in the question will not happen, taking the meaning 'I doubt'; (3) in other cases, 'taha' is interpreted as 'I wonder', 'I express doubt as to...'; while (4) in imperatives,

---

2. Λεξιλογική βάση δεδομένων κυπριακής διαλέκτου [Lexicography of the Cypriot dialect, database]: http://lexcy.library.ucy.ac.cy/

3. When 'taha' carries the meaning of apparently, it is associated with hearsay.

Chapter 8

'taha' could be equivalent to 'pretend to perform A' or 'I doubt indirectly that P' or 'I do not really ask you to perform A'. Those interpretations lead to the conclusion that in imperatives, 'taha' is an indirect request that the interlocutor should merely pretend to make. Finding Pavlidou's (1989) account of 'taha' problematic, Ifantidou (2000) argues that there is little evidence on the semantic nature of 'taha' in that study as well as insufficient analysis on the double function of the word (which is sometimes interpreted as an evidential particle and sometimes as a hearsay particle). Based on Wilson and Sperber's (1994) relevance theory[4], she proposes an alternative analysis, in which:

> "taha is a procedural marker which directly encodes weak evidential information, i.e. something like the meaning 'it seems'. As a weak evidential, it affects the strength of the assumption communicated (and hence the recommended degree of commitment to the proposition expressed). The hearsay, and other implicatures communicated, are pragmatically derived from its evidential meaning. On its hearsay interpretation, it makes the ground-floor assertion to which it is attached as a case of interpretive rather than descriptive use. In both cases, it alters the truth-conditional status of the ground-floor assertion to which is attached and will be perceived as making an essential contribution to truth conditions. Which interpretation (evidential or hearsay) the hearer is intended to recover, or does in fact recover, is determined by considerations of the relevance" (p. 120).

In a later research, Ifantidou (2005, pp. 386-387) concluded that the evidentials that are more complex from a syntactic point of view (i.e. 'it seems that/to me') are acquired earlier than the evidentials which are syntactically less complex (i.e. 'τάχα'/ 'δήθεν'). Extending Ifantidou's (2001) conception,

---

4. Relevance theory (Wilson & Sperber, 1994) is a cognitive approach, according to which the communication process involves: a) encoding, transfer, and decoding of messages, and b) other elements, including inference and context. In order to understand and interpret an utterance, the hearer needs not only to know the meaning(s) of a sentence/word. On the contrary he/she needs to infer what was implicitly conveyed, to decide if the utterance was literally, metaphorically, or ironically intended etc. Thus, "every utterance creates an expectation of relevance in the hearer, with the preferred interpretation being the one that best satisfies that expectation of relevance" (Wilson & Sperber, 1994, p. 85). The information is relevant to the hearer if it interacts in a certain way with his/her existing assumptions about the world. The new information may confirm or strengthen his/her existing assumptions. In cases where the new assumption contradicts the old one, the weaker is abandoned.

Tsiplakou and Papapetrou (2020) reached the conclusion that some functions are shared between the Cypriot-Greek 'taha' and the Standard Greek 'taha'. More specifically, in both varieties, 'taha' functions as an evidential/hearsay particle, disputing the factuality of the proposition. In questions, it has the function of 'maybe' and 'perhaps', while in imperatives it is equivalent to 'pretend to'. Moreover, in declaratives, 'taha' does not necessarily express a dissociative speaker's attitude but carries out an evidential/hearsay function, related to the speaker's attitude toward the source of the evidence. 'Taha mou' (τάχα μου) (a variation of 'taha') in declaratives indicates that the speaker does not endorse the truth or the factuality of the proposition in its scope.

Apart from the above-mentioned functions, shared in the two Greek varieties, the researchers showed convincingly that the Cypriot 'taha' has some extra functions, since it can be a pragmatic marker of dissociation, not from the propositional content, but from associated implicatures, therefore 'taha' is non-truth functional. In addition, their study revealed that in questions, 'taha' functions as a marker used by the speaker to ask of the interlocutor to expand on and clarify his/her statement, while simultaneously he/she questions the validity of the possible explanations. Moreover, in imperatives, in some cases 'taha' is related to clarifications only at first blush, while it's substantial function is to indicate a repetition of the interlocutor's utterance by the speaker. Focusing on the 'young taha' (used mainly by adolescents) the researchers claimed that it is not just mere filler used for conversational purposes. On the contrary, it could be considered as an innovative speech mark since it can only be found in youth speech. Consequently, 'young taha' is not as different as it seems to adult 'taha'. Based on the above, the researchers concluded that Cypriot 'taha' (both in its 'adult' and 'young' version) has a metarepresentational use, namely it marks the use of the proposition in its scope (a set of implicatures of the proposition expressed, which the speaker does not endorse) as attributive or metarepresentational. Thus, 'taha' allows for suspended speaker commitment or non-endorsement. Furthermore, 'taha' indicates a metarepresentational use of the speaker's own utterances and thoughts. Based on the above-mentioned, the researchers suggested the investigation of a full semantic 'bleaching' of 'taha' over time.

1.2. The phenomenon of language change

The phenomenon of language change happens macroscopically, and it is a universal, normal, and continuous process, resulting in all languages. The effect of social factors on language change have been proven by sociolinguistic theories (Lyons, 2001, pp. 204, 234-240), shedding light on the phenomenon as a part of the wider natural world change, not as a matter of progress or of the language fading away (Aitchison, 2001, p. 4). On the contrary, Nikiforidou (2002, p. 102) points out that the language of a generation is never the same with the language of the previous or the following generations.

In light of the above, the students' frequent use of 'taha', while speaking the Cypriot-Greek dialect, and its several contextual functions were noted and researched by the author during the past two years. The research question is as follows: how many and what functions does 'taha' take in the participants' Cypriot-Greek oral speech?

2. Method

2.1. The participants

Twenty-nine first-year university students of the Cyprus University of Technology Language Centre participated in the research. The 29 participants were 17 males and 12 females. Apart from one student of Greek origin, the rest of the participants were all Cypriot-Greeks, having the Cypriot-Greek dialect as their mother-tongue.

2.2. Data collection

The current study was conducted during a period of 13 weeks. The aim was to examine the pragmatic functions of the Cypriot-Greek 'taha' as it was used in the field of classroom discourse. The students were informed of the researcher's intention to study their oral interaction in classroom discourse, without being given any details about the focus of inquiry to avoid influencing their speech. The next step involved describing the method the researcher intended to follow (video recordings and field notes), as it is proposed by Baynham (2002, p. 320) and Filias (2003, pp. 97-98). The second step involved the students signing a consent form for their participation in the research and being informed about the ethics behind the study. In order to confront the problems created by IRE/F scheme (Chafi, Elkhouzai, & Arhlam, 2014, p. 103), the 32 critical episodes included in the research were drawn from the parts of 18 lessons called '10 minutes of free discussion'. During that time, the students were given the opportunity to discuss lesson-related issues.

The researcher's role in this process was restricted, participating in the discussion only after she was called by the students. Lessons were video-recorded, and three hours of oral speech were collected out of which 32 critical episodes were isolated. Then, a questionnaire that incorporated the 32 critical episodes in their context (the phrase included 'taha' and both its previous and next phrase, accompanied by the topic of the conversation) was developed by the author. The students were asked to note the functions of 'taha' according to their opinion, by answering 'open-ended questions' (Filias, 2003, pp. 147, 154-155). The post-questionnaire data analysis discussion aimed to help students interpret the functions they had attributed to 'taha' during the questionnaire completion.

3. Results and discussion

Data analysis revealed that 'taha' appeared 35 times in the 32 critical episodes that were isolated from the three hour oral exchanges, having several functions according to the context.

3.1. Indicative results of the questionnaire

The questionnaire was given intentionally to the 29 participants in order to ascertain how the users themselves interpret their own language choices. The

Chapter 8

participants interpreted the functions of 'taha' in their own utterances using the following: 'no meaning' (in 30 critical episodes, 336 times), 'allegedly/supposedly' (in 28 critical episodes, 163 times), 'for example/let's say' (in 29 critical episodes, 145 times), 'namely/that is to say' (in 16 critical episodes, 81 times), 'namely?/what do you mean?' (in 16 critical episodes, 81 times), 'that' (in 4 critical episodes, 39 times), 'in order to' (in 5 critical episodes, 35 times), 'emphasis' (in 6 critical episodes, 27 times), 'certainty' (in 2 critical episodes, 9 times). They all interpreted 'tzie taha?' as 'so what?' What is interesting is that they ascribed to 'taha' several functions depended on the contexts and more specifically, depended on their attitudes/thoughts toward the propositional content or the associated implicatures.

3.2. Indicative content discussion post-questionnaire completion

After the questionnaire completion by the students, an interesting discussion unfolded. Most of the interpretations of 'taha' as a word devoid of content (as it was stated in the questionnaire 336 times) were recanted, by phrases/words such as 'lack of certainty', 'disbelief', 'irony', 'indifference', 'unawareness'. Also, many of the questionnaire's statements were enlightened, e.g. the participants explained that they used 'taha?' as equivalent to 'namely?' (δηλαδή;), as a word that asks from the interlocutor to proceed to clarifications or explanations. Regarding their statements that 'taha' somehow works as 'that is to say/namely/for example', an assertion emerged: in specific contexts, 'taha' works as a hedging device, 'protecting' the speaker from potential face-threatening acts.

Another interesting fact is that many of the students mentioned they used 'taha' in an incompatible way, which they found to be very amusing. Among their reactions were "Oh my God! I say 'taha' with no reason!", "I don't know why I said 'taha', it doesn't make sense", "I wanted to say 'must', 'taha' means that I don't believe him". This is probably due to the fact that the participants were influenced by the power of the dictionaries and the meanings they ascribed to it.

3.3. The results of the pragmatic analysis

A deeper analysis based on the method proposed by Tsiplakou and Papapetrou (2020) proves that not only did the participants use 'taha' in a compatible way, ascribing to it several pragmatic functions, but they indeed used it based on (1) the desirable speech acts they wanted to perform, and (2) their own attitudes/ thoughts toward the propositional content or the associated implicatures.

Table 1. Conversation about students' duties in group work

S1	Γιατί εμ με έπκιαες τηλέφωνον εχτές; Why didn't you call me yesterday?
S2	Είπεν μου ο Μάριος **τάχα** εν ημπορείς. Marios told me **taha** you can't.
S1	Όι μάνα μου... Oh, my God...

In the above utterance (Table 1), S1 asks her interlocutor S2 why he did not call her the previous day (to study together). He answers that he did not because Marios told him that 'taha' she could not study with him. Assuming that 'taha' is used by S2 implying that Marios lied to him is problematic, since almost all the participants stated in the questionnaire and during the discussion that Marios indeed told the truth. Considering the above, 'taha' can be seen as a pragmatic marker of dissociation (not from the propositional content) but from associated implicatures, connected to the suspicion of S2 that S1 intentionally let Marios believing that she could not study with S2 (insincerity). Another potential analysis is that 'taha' works as a hedging device, 'protecting' the speaker (S2) and mitigating potentially face-threatening acts (see Tsiplakou & Papapetrou, 2020, 'young taha'). In other words, it could be interpreted as an index through which the speaker (S2) excuses himself for not calling S1. This 'bipolarity' indicates that these examples need further investigation.

Table 2. Conversation about the decoding of the 'hidden meanings' in a journalistic article

S1	Κυρία, **τάχα** τζείνον με τα «κρυμμένα νοήματα» εν το κατάλαβα. Mrs., I didn't understand **taha** the part with the 'hidden meanings'.

T	Θυμηθείτε τον Τριβιζά τζαι το αόρατον πράσινον καγκουρό του.
	Please remember Triviza and his green invisible kangaroo.
S2	**Τάχα** οι αόρατες λέξεις; Να μπουν τούτον;
	Taha the 'invisible words'? What is that?
T	Να ξαναδούμεν τον Τριβιζάν;
	Shall we study again Triviza?

In Table 2, the first speaker uses 'taha' as a marker requesting a clarification regarding the 'hidden meanings', therefore' taha does not work as an evidential/hearsay particle, or as a marker of dissociation from the propositional content. On the contrary, it seems that it works as a shield protecting the speaker from being 'exposed' for not understanding the 'hidden meanings' (face-threatening acts). Consequently, it works as a hedging device. The second 'taha' included in the contribution of S2 implies that what follows (the 'invisible words?') is possibly the answer to S1 query and, at the same time, it is connected to his teacher scaffolding, "Please remember Triviza and his green invisible kangaroo". Simultaneously, the question mark at the end of the phrase ("Taha the invisible words?") in combination to the later question, "What is that?", indicates that 'taha' works as a hedging device, expressing hesitation, protecting S2's face from a possible wrong connection between the 'hidden meanings' and the 'invisible words', and waiting for a confirmation by the teacher while he is not sure what the 'invisible words' are.

Table 3. Conversation about the strategies used in order to discover the irrational purpose in a journalistic article

S1	Ποιος έβαλες ότι εν ο σκοπός του αρθρογράφου;
	What did you write as the writer's purpose?
S2	Ότι **τάχα** η πόμπα στην Βόρειον Κορέαν εν επικίνδυνη.
	That **taha** the bomb in South Korea is dangerous.

The above utterance in Table 3 is quite impressive, considering that most of the participants stated, both in the questionnaire and discussion, that the speaker wanted to indicate that the bomb in South Korea is indeed dangerous. Most of them confirmed that 'taha' is a marker of emphasis to the speaker's attitude toward the propositional content. Considering the factuality of the proposition, it is more than obvious that 'taha' is not a hearsay particle, it does not work as a hedging device, nor as a marker of dissociation from the associated implicatures. On the contrary, it works as a marker that emphasises the propositional content, rendering it as completely factual. The speaker is totally committed to the factuality of the proposition and expresses his agreement to the writer's purpose. This function of 'taha' (a marker of emphasis to the propositional content) has not been recorded in the bibliography so far, thus, it brings a new function to the surface.

Table 4. Conversation about the power and the influence of the media

T	Θέλεις να μοιραστείς μαζί μας την εμπειρία σου από την ομιλία που πήγες; Would you like to share with us your experience from the speech you attended?
S	Εμ μου άρεσεν καθόλου. Επέμενεν ότι **τάχα** το ραδιόφωνον επηρεάζει παραπάνω που την τηλεόρασην. I didn't like it at all. He (the speaker) was insisting that **taha** radio influences more than television.

Filling out the questionnaire, the participants ascribed to 'taha' the function of 'supposedly/allegedly', the function of a marker of disagreement to the propositional content and stated that it is a word devoid of content. Analysing this critical episode (Table 4), it is obvious that 'taha' works as a marker of the speaker's dissociation from the propositional content, disputing the factuality of the proposition ("radio influences [people] more than television"). Besides, this is supported by the previous utterance, which expressed the speaker's discontent with the speech he had attended.

Table 5. Conversation about the difficulties of academic writing

S1	Πάντως η κυρία Αντρέου είπεν ότι **τάχα** είμαστεν οι καλλύττεροι που τ' άλλα group. Mrs. Andreou said that **taha** we are better than the other groups.
S2	Επήαμεν τα καλλύττερα, κυρία! We did better, Mrs!

According to the participants, the speaker in the above utterance uses 'taha' to emphasise the statement given by the lecturer (Table 5). The latter acknowledged that the specific group, including the speaker, had a better performance than the other groups. Some other participants considered 'taha' as an index of certainty from the speaker's part, regarding the meaning of the statement. Analysing the above critical episode, from a pragmatic point of view, undoubtedly, 'taha' emphasises the speaker's agreement to the propositional content and the associated implicatures.

Table 6. Conversation regarding the date of the midterm exam

T	Την επόμενην βδομάδαν εννά 'χουμεν την ενδιάμεσην μας. Next week we will have our midterm exam.
S1	Μα κυρία έχουμεν ενδιάμεση με τον Στυλιανού. But, Mrs. we have a midterm with Stilianou.
S2	**Τζιαι τάχα;** Εν ημπορούμεν να τα κάμουμεν τζιαι τα θκυο; Να ποσπαζούμαστεν. **Tzie taha?** Can we do both? To get it over with.
T	Θα το συζητήσουμεν. We shall speak about this.

It is important to note that, while the participants were filling in the questionnaire, they interpreted 'tzie taha?' as a marker of disagreement to the previous utterance of S1 or as a marker of irony, considering 'tzie taha?' as equivalent to 'so what?' (Table 6). It is obvious that 'tzie taha?' works as a marker of dissociation not from the propositional content (The following week the students have a midterm exam in another lesson), but from the associated implicatures in S1's utterance. S2 ironically disputes S1's implicature that it is not feasible for the students to have two midterm exams in the same week, while he rejects in advance any possible argumentation/explanation. Besides, what follows ("Can we do both? To get it over with") strengthens this function of 'tzie taha?'.

Table 7. Conversation for the preparation of the students prior to the lesson

S1	Έπρεπεν **τάχα** να θκιαβάσουμεν ούλλον το PowerPoint. We **taha** should have studied all the PowerPoint.
S2	Είπεν μας έτσι πράμαν; Did she say such a thing?
S3	Ναι, στο προηγούμενον μάθημαν. Yes, in the previous lesson.

The participants statements in the questionnaire about the specific function of 'taha' were various: 'namely', 'supposedly/allegedly', an index of obligation, an index of disagreement, and an index of emphasis to the propositional content are those with the highest frequency. However, considering that the students were, indeed, assigned with the specific presentation prior to the lesson, it is obvious that 'taha' cannot work as a dissociative from the propositional content, nor as an evidential/hearsay particle, indicating that the speaker does not endorse the factuality of the proposition. On the contrary, it works as a hedging device, protecting the speaker's face from threatening acts (i.e. to be exposed that she did not study the whole PowerPoint). What is interesting is that, when the specific student (S1) was later asked if she had studied the whole PowerPoint, she admitted to not studying even a slide of it (Table 7).

Data analysis also revealed the placing of 'taha' at the beginning, in the middle, and at the end of sentences. Furthermore, when 'taha' appeared in sentences which had the illocutionary force of a question, no participant interpreted it as carrying no meaning but as a marker through which the speaker asks the interlocutor to expand or clarify his/her statement (see also Tsiplakou & Papapetrou, 2020) – sometimes disputing possible clarifications/explanations, but sometimes in a neutral attitude towards them. Finally, what should also be mentioned is the fact that, even though the students were neither aware of the speech acts theory (Austin, 1962), or of the relevance theory (Sperber & Wilson, 1986), in most cases they interpreted 'taha' based on its function in specific contexts, and they attributed to it (among others) the following: "It shows irony", "It stresses the meaning of the sentence", "It is equivalent to 'namely'", "Taha means for example", "Taha stresses the purpose of the speaker", "Taha shows certainty", "In this case 'taha' is the same as uncertainty".

4. Conclusions

There is little literature concerning 'taha' in Cypriot-Greek dialect (Papapetrou, 2017; Tsiplakou & Papapetrou, 2020). In the current research, the participants used 'taha' in Cypriot-Greek oral speech frequently and spontaneously, deploying its several functions depending on the context. During the conversation that followed the completion of the questionnaire, most of the participants changed their first interpretations of 'taha' into different ones. Probably the differentiation between the first (in questionnaire) and the second (in discussion) interpretation of 'taha' is connected to the fact that the participants spontaneously use 'taha', choosing one of its functions that is suitable to their attitudes/thoughts toward the propositional content or to the associated implicatures, but in their mind, the basic meaning that the dictionaries ascribe to 'taha' ('supposedly/allegedly') is more dominant. Another interesting conclusion is that out of 32 critical episodes, only three included 'taha' as a dissociative, non-endorsing of the truth or the factuality of the proposition. Briefly, 'taha' functions as a marker of dissociation from the associated implicatures, as a hedging device mitigating potential face-threatening acts, as a marker that requests clarifications/explanations regarding a previous utterance, and as a marker of dissociation from the propositional content. The above-mentioned conclusions agree with a previous study by Tsiplakou and Papapetrou (2020), according to which 'taha' marks the use of the proposition in its scope as attributive or metarepresentational. In the current research, 'tzie taha?' appears to work as a marker disputing the factuality of the proposition, implying an ironical attitude to it and being dissociative from the implicatures connected to the proposition. Finally, in the current study an additional function of 'taha' was revealed: in some contexts, it works as an index of emphasis to the propositional content, while in some other contexts it emphasises the associated implicatures. Considering this study as exploratory, it is believed that more research is needed.

5. Acknowledgements

I wish to thank the students who participated in the current research.

References

Aitchison, J. (2001). *Language change: progress or decay* (3rd ed.). Cambridge University Press.

Austin, J. L. (1962). *How to do things with words*. Clarendon Press.
Baynham, M. (2002). Πρακτικές γραμματισμού. Μετάφ. Μ. Αραποπούλου [Literacy practices. Translated by M. Arapopoulou]. Metehmio.
Cazden, C. B. (1988). *Classroom discourse: the language of teaching and learning.* Heinemann.
Chafi, M. E., Elkhouzai, E., & Arhlam, A. (2014). The dynamic of classroom talk in modern primary school: towards dialogic pedagogy. *International Journal of Education and Research, 2*(5), 99-114. http://ijern.com/journal/May-2014/10.pdf
Charalambakis, C. G. (2014). Χρηστικό λεξικό της νεοελληνικής γλώσσας [The utilitarian dictionary of Modern Greek]. Academy of Athens, National Printing House.
Filias, V. (2003). Εισαγωγή στη μεθοδολογία και τις τεχνικές των κοινωνικών ερευνών [Introduction to methodology and techniques of the social researches]. Gutenberg.
Hadjioannou, K. (2000). Ετυμολογικό λεξικό της ομιλουμένης κυπριακής διαλέκτου [Etymological dictionary of the spoken Cypriot dialect] (2nd ed.). Tamassos.
Hadjipieris, I., & Kapatas, O. (2015). Κοινό Λεξικό Της Ελληνοκυπριακής και Τουρκοκυπριακής Διαλέκτου (Ιστορικό – Ετυμολογικό), Kıbrıs Rum ve Türk Diyalektlerinin Ortak Sözlüğü (Tarihi ve Etimolojik) [Joint dictionary of the Greek-Cypriot and the Turkish Cypriot dialect (historical- terminological)].
Ifantidou, E. (2000). Procedural encoding of explicatures by the Modern Greek particle taha. In G. Andersen & T. Fretheim (Eds), *Pragmatic markers and propositional attitude* (pp. 119-144). John Benjamin. https://doi.org/10.1075/pbns.79.06ifa
Ifantidou, E. (2001). *Evidentials and relevance*. John Benjamins.
Ifantidou, E. (2005). Pragmatics, cognition and asymmetrically acquired evidentials. *Pragmatics, 15*(4), 369-394. https://doi.org/10.1075/prag.15.4.04ifa
Institute of Modern Greek Studies. (2003). Λεξικό της κοινής νεοελληνικής [Dictionary of common Greek language]. Aristotle University of Thessaloniki.
Lyons, J. (2001). *Εισαγωγή στη γλωσσολογία* [Introduction to linguistics (8th ed.) translated by M. Arampopoulou, M. Vrahionidou, A. Archakis & A. Karra]. Pataki.
Mpampiniotis, G. (2002). Λεξικό της νέας ελληνικής γλώσσας [Dictionary of Modern Greek Language] (2nd ed.). Lexicology Centre.
Nikiforidou, K. (2002). Γλωσσική αλλαγή [Language change]. In A. F. Christides (Ed.), *The history of the Greek language* (pp 102-107). Institute of Modern Greek Studies [Manolis Triandaphyllidis Foundation].

Papaggelou, P. (2001). *Το κυπριακό ιδίωμα. Μέγα κυπρο-ελληνο-αγγλικό (και με λατινική ορολογία) λεξικό* [The Cypriot idiom. Great Cypriot-Greek-English (including Latin terminology) dictionary]. Iolkos.

Papapetrou, C. (2017). *The Cypriot Greek particle taha*. MA Dissertation. Open University of Cyprus.

Pavlidou, T. (1989). Particles, pragmatics and other. *Selected papers on theoretical and applied linguistics, 3*, 315-343. http://ejournals.lib.auth.gr/thal/article/view/7180

Petrides, G. (2016). *Η γλώσσα των Κυπρίων και της εκκλησίας* [The language of the Cypriots and the church]. Petrides.

Sperber, D., & Wilson. D. (1986). *Relevance: communication and cognition*. Basil Blackwell.

Triantaphyllides, M. (1978). *Νεοελληνική γραμματική (της δημοτικής)* [Modern Greek grammar (of Demotic)]. Aristotle University of Thessaloniki, Institute of Modern Greek Studies, Manolis Triantaphyllides Foundation.

Tsiplakou, S., & Papapetrou, C. (2020). *Two dialects, one particle—taha?* [white paper]. https://www.academia.edu/43265788/Two_dialects_one_particle_taha

Tzartzanos, A. (1953). *Νεοελληνική σύνταξις (της κοινής δημοτικής)* [Modern Greek syntax (of the Common Demotic)]. OESB.

Wilson, D., & Sperber, D. (1994). Outline of the relevance theory. *Links & Letters*, 85-106. https://ddd.uab.cat/pub/lal/11337397n1/11337397n1p85.pdf

Yiangoullis, C. G. (2002). *Θησαυρός κυπριακής διαλέκτου. Ερμηνευτικός και ετυμολογικός από τον 13ο αι. μέχρι σήμερα* [Thesaurus of the Greek Cypriot dialect. Interpretative and etymological from the 13th c. until today]. Yiangoullis.

Yiangoullis, C. G. (2009). *Θησαυρός κυπριακής διαλέκτου. Ερμηνευτικό, ετυμολογικό, φρασεολογικό και ονοματολογικό λεξικό της μεσαιωνικής και νεότερης κυπριακής διαλέκτου* [Thesaurus of the Greek Cypriot dialect. Interpretative, etymological, phraseological, and nomenclature dictionary of the medieval and modern Cypriot dialect]. Theopress.

Yiangoullis, C. G. (2014). *Θησαυρός της μεσαιωνικής και νεότερης κυπριακής διαλέκτου* [Thesaurus of medieval and modern Cypriot dialect]. Yiangoullis.

Author index

C
Charalambous, Theodora vi, 4, 65

E
Efthimiou, Fotini vi, 5, 151

G
Giannikas, Christina Nicole v, vi, 1, 4, 65

H
Hadjiconstantinou, Stavroulla vi, 3, 29
Hubbard, Philip v, xi

K
Kakoulli Constantinou, Elis v, vi, 1, 4, 89
Korai, Maria vi, 3, 7
Kosmas, Panagiotis vii, 4, 133

N
Nicolaou, Anna vii, 4, 111

P
Papadima-Sophocleous, Salomi v, vii, 1, 3, 4, 7, 65, 89

S
Soulé, María Victoria vii, 3, 47

www.ingramcontent.com/pod-product-compliance
Lightning Source LLC
Chambersburg PA
CBHW022010160426
43197CB00007B/374